Praise for
THE BEAUTY WORLD THROUGH THE LENS OF A PSYCHIATRIST

"A medical doctor by day and a beauty consultant by night? Say what? How? Jane, in her clear, matter-of-fact writing, makes sense of this 'dual life.' She explains the similarities and differences between her vocation and avocation with clarity and humor."

—Diane Kwitnicki, educational consultant

"This memoir is a fascinating glimpse into the life of Dr. Sofair and her approach to medicine, psychiatry, and the overall human experience. I can relate to many of the decisions Jane has had to make in her life—from overcoming a tragedy in the community like Sandy Hook to navigating the perils of running a small business and private practice in a rapidly changing healthcare business environment. Her professional life is nicely woven into personal experience to remind us that physicians are indeed human, and how we attempt to heal others is often therapeutic to ourselves."

—John Rimmer, DO, former chief medical officer, Carepoint Health

"In this memoir of moonlighting as a beauty consultant, psychiatrist Jane Sofair offers an alluring how-to manual for anyone who has dreamed of breaking free of professional and societal expectations in search of self-realization and work-life balance."

—Elizabeth Shakman Hurd, Northwestern University

"Life is nothing short of complex when more than one thing can be true simultaneously. Too many people want to one-dimensionalize our fellow man instead of allowing others to freely explore life's many facets. Sofair eloquently and brilliantly expresses how to break out of life's norms and expectations and embrace many sides within one person. An excellent autobiography!"

—Alexys Vaulkenroth Wolf, author, publisher, minister, and founder of The Fiery Sword Global Ministries

"In her new memoir, Dr Jane Sofair engages the audience by explaining her unique career trajectory with wit and translucence. In doing so, she enlivens the sometimes-gray trials and tribulations of medical care with a full-hue palette of creativity. A must read for anyone considering medicine or another potentially high-burnout helping profession!"

—Naomi Weinshenker, MD, psychiatrist, journalist, contributing freelance writer for Psychologytoday.com

"Jane Sofair has written a compelling memoir . . . Seeking relief from career burnout, she expanded her identity as a seasoned psychiatrist by becoming a part-time salesperson in beauty retail, a vastly different skill set. This memoir is a must-read and a powerful inspiration for anyone contemplating a mid-life career redirection . . . I thoroughly enjoyed and highly recommend this book."

—Barbara Bartlik, MD, author and editor of *Integrative Sexual Health* and associate director of the Women's Health Collaborative, Mental Health Division

"Dr. Jane Sofair's memoir has taken me on a journey of her early years as a student of psychiatry through her honest and heartfelt struggles as a respected psychiatrist later in her life, who wanted something different in her professional career. I identified with her struggles within the challenging environment of health care today. Jane was able to express her doubts and challenges clearly, while uncovering what it was like to try a completely different profession than psychiatry. I could see that she . . . called upon her psychiatry skills within the beauty realm to help her understand and thrive in that world. I highly recommend this read for those searching for a change in their career."

—Karen Shea, RN, value analysis consultant

"How sad that corporate entities have intervened in the demands fulfilling our professional obligations to the patients we see. Dr. Sofair's writing focuses on these issues in a most insightful and empathetic way. The modality of being a 'good' psychiatrist is now measured by quantity rather than quality. How fortunate for her to have extended her talents to another field that also requires a high degree of insight and sensitivity. Her book is both refreshing and inspirational in the way she has combined 'beauty' as a component of 'wellness.'"

—Harvey Hammer, MD, chair emeritus of psychiatry, Morristown Medical Center, Atlantic Health

"*The Beauty World Through the Lens of a Psychiatrist* is an interesting and fun read. Jane's descriptions of her life's journey and career choices are heartfelt, honest, and very relatable. I particularly enjoyed her sense of humor and humility as she wrote about the transition from her daytime profession of a prestigious doctor to her nighttime venture of a successful beauty consultant and the challenge of integrating as well as separating the two professions."

—Patricia Berdela, RN

"In *The Beauty World Through the Lens of a Psychiatrist*, Dr. Sofair invites readers into a unique and deeply personal exploration of the beauty industry. Her perspective, tinged with eccentric charm, transforms a passion into a secondary career that both intrigues and inspires. This book is a delightfully unconventional journey into the intersection of science and beauty."

—Mary Gorman, Intentional Living Coaching

"Everyone has an unusual story, and Jane has written about hers in these pages. Not only has she persisted as an accomplished psychiatrist, but she has also ventured out to become a skillful beauty consultant. Her diverse choices are unique and can encourage you to venture out and try something new for yourself. The two professions are so opposite, yet, Jane's examples of her experiences bring together how skills in both areas interact with each other. Excellent read."

—Susan Hattem Celi, independent senior sales director in the beauty and cosmetics field

"It is useful to view any profession through the lens of another one; it is particularly enlightening to do so from professions as divergent as psychiatry and beauty consultancy. Dr. Jane Sofair does just that for her reader. Her self-reflection helps answer questions that arise for anyone—when do we change career paths? How do we resist the destructive power of burn out? How do we use the lessons of one career to inform a new one? I recommend *The Beauty World Through the Lens of a*

Psychiatrist for anyone interested in learning about either of these career paths. I also recommend this book for anyone who wants to read of a life informed by resilience and intelligence."

> —R. Barbara Gitenstein, PhD, author of *Portrait of a Presidency: My Life as President of the College of New Jersey* and president emerita, the College of New Jersey

"A lot of writers can describe but very few can put you there. Jane Sofair—through her pure brilliance of teasing necessary detail and the nostalgia that comes along with it—is one of the best storytellers out there right now. Everything is refreshingly unexpected. The crafted words make you reflect on personal strength and what it means to be grounded. That said, Sofair writes for everyone. She has democratized the art of words to the bare bone essentials of the human heart beating at its most inherent pace. A must, must read!"

> —Kip Langton, author of *Hell of Hosanna* and *Victorian Stillness*

"A many-faceted memoir, Jane Sofair's *The Beauty World Through the Lens of a Psychiatrist* is much more than skin deep. Working as a beauty consultant on the side, Jane soon recognizes the parallels between the two professions and discovers that being a beauty consultant is another way to touch people's lives. With an engaging narrative, and an invitation to think outside the box, this inspiring account is packed with advice, intriguing facts, and a brief history lesson on the world of beauty. This is a perfect read for anyone who wants to step out of their comfort zone and is considering an add-on career."

> —Jennifer Artley, author of *Improvising in Italian*

The Beauty World Through the Lens of a Psychiatrist
by Jane B. Sofair

© Copyright 2025 Jane B. Sofair

ISBN 979-8-88824-720-4

All rights reserved. No part of this publication may be reproduced, stored in a retrieval system, or transmitted in any form or by any means—electronic, mechanical, photocopy, recording, or any other—except for brief quotations in printed reviews, without the prior written permission of the author.

Published by

3705 Shore Drive
Virginia Beach, VA 23455
800-435-4811
www.koehlerbooks.com

THE *Beauty World* THROUGH THE LENS OF A *Psychiatrist*

JANE B. SOFAIR

VIRGINIA BEACH
CAPE CHARLES

Dedicated to every hardworking professional
and every hardworking person.
Always embrace possibility.

Jane Sofair, age 23, as a medical student

You can't be a puppy as a writer.
—Sir Martin Louis Amis, 1949–2023

PREFACE

The inspiration to write *The Beauty World Through the Lens of a Psychiatrist* was probably there from the beginning when I signed on as a beauty consultant around the year 2013. I kept reverting back to the work of the late Barbara Ehrenreich, an investigative journalist, who spent time traveling around the country as an incognito blue-collar employee. Ms. Ehrenreich subsequently recorded her impressions of a different America in her book, *Nickel and Dimed*. It all seemed so romantic and adventurous, to work on another side in a completely different capacity from your day job. And I believed that I was wired to give it a try, in this case within the beauty industry, given an enduring commitment to being stylish along with having an easy way of relating to people.

The question I would continually ask myself once the beauty consulting contract had been signed was whether to go public with the new enterprise or keep it close to the vest, mainly in the interest of being taken seriously as a psychiatrist. No one could possibly have had that answer nor have been able to advise me on what to do because, frankly, this dual circumstance was as foreign to them as it was to me. People's reactions would vary, ranging from an eyebrow raise to an empathetic but stretched and holistic spin on my new project, literally bridging the mind with the body, the psyche with the external appearance. And the endorsers would believe that it was precisely my psychiatric background that would enable me to be an effective beauty consultant. They saw the connection.

But for me, entry into the beauty world felt at best precarious, fluctuating between exhilaration and absurdity. To a certain extent, I would have to toughen up and discipline myself to be oblivious to others' judgment. I would have to be able to step outside of my habitually cautious, measured nature, and leap forth. I had observed this among makeup artists, cosmetic specialists at department store counters, and my newly formed group of beauty consulting peers.

Logic dictated that everyone in my solar system would adjust. They would have to, and they would be there to support me. Plus, I would learn from them. Their feedback would be welcomed, accepted as constructive. Through honest trial and error, I would adapt the most effective selling and promotional strategies.

Early on, the sales motto "No means yes" caught my eye. "No means yes?" I laughed over the telephone with a friend one evening. There must have been something I missed behind this counterintuitive and amusing statement. But within the sales culture, the idea was that if a prospective customer initially declined your services, you would then pitch the offer again in a manner they couldn't refuse; a win-win strategy for everyone. Now, the customer could not wait to sit down with you for a beauty appointment. They had reconsidered, and you hoped they would eventually become your loyal customer as long as you remained nonchalant yet caring in your demeanor.

Over time, however, I grew to doubt this notion. "No" definitely meant "no." Sometimes it felt like being slapped across the face, like the few times I made follow up calls after enthusiastically networking, only to have the prospective customer who had eagerly accepted my business card and samples the preceding evening during the cocktail hour, hang up. Or the half dozen times that customers did not appear for their initial booking—there I sat, waiting, feeling like a total loser. It was during those private, awkward moments, that I repeatedly asked myself what I was trying to prove by being a beauty consultant. Why was I putting up with this level of embarrassment? I should just quit and stay on as a full-time doctor. In some ways, being a physician felt so much safer than being a beauty consultant. Within the field of medicine, there was far more structure and predictability along with built-in safeguards for the provider, like an expectation of the patient's adherence to your appointment schedule, adherence to your recommendations, and, of course, expectation of payment.

And yet, the additional source of income from a beauty business was most seductive. Sales commissions could serve as a financial safety net and potentially augment spending money. It was generally known that there were big dollars to be made in the cosmetics industry. Some of the highly successful sales directors were easily making six-figure incomes. How did I know this? It was public information, posted in the company's monthly magazine, along with their glamorous headshots. Recognition and wealth apparently came easily to these sales directors if they were willing to put in their time and accept the risk of all those rejections that came with their success.

I really enjoyed some of the other consultants. I cannot exactly say that they became family, as that would sound inauthentic, but they certainly energized me in ways unique to the sales world with their unbridled optimism. Their motto? "Just keep going." If prospective customers are not interested, then it's their loss, not yours. Nothing in sales is ever personal. The other beauty consultants were generally friendly and kind, taking people at their word rather than probing into deeper meanings. They did not necessarily overthink or overanalyze. They were quick to laugh, and, in general, kept things light.

They were nonjudgmental. They rarely asked me about psychiatry or my clinical cases. We stuck to our shared world of sales strategies and amusing anecdotes, sometimes positively intoxicating, their resilience contagious!

Then there was the burnout factor. Had I become a beauty consultant as an antidote to physician burnout? I never thought of myself as burned out, maybe a little weary. In truth, I am not even crazy about the term "burnout" because it implies a personal deficit and is therefore laden with stigma. Most doctors view themselves as highly successful professionals.

The reality is that professional stress among physicians has conceptually evolved into a systemic issue rather than an individual shortcoming, partially addressed with lifestyle advice like adhering to a balanced diet and routine exercise. In a 2022 letter to the American Medical Association membership, Dr. Gerald E. Harmon, then president, wrote "As a veteran and a family doctor, I have seen what trauma looks like firsthand. It doesn't take a trained eye, though, to recognize that physicians are struggling. The COVID-19 pandemic has exacerbated existing problems within our health care system that limit our ability to do our jobs and can threaten patient safety. Physician burnout, prior authorization, inappropriate scope of practice expansions, telehealth access—there are so many challenges to overcome. . ."

This brings me to another point. I say this with the utmost of respect for my colleagues, in questioning whether solo psychiatric practice as a business model is ultimately viable in this rapidly ever-evolving healthcare environment. Unless, of course, you are prepared to adhere to a strict fee-for-service model. There are just too many rolling expenses, regulations, technical advances, insurance and coding requirements, and high patient expectations for one single physician to handle. I speak from experience.

In 2007, when I decided to leave a locum tenens assignment

to jump back into solo private practice for the second time, my director at the site interjected a note of caution, adding "You have to be so incredibly business savvy these days to pull off your own solo practice. Are you sure you want this, Dr. Sofair?" And that was during the year 2007, when the healthcare arena was far less complex than it is today.

Circling back to what I hope you gain from my memoir, there is not necessarily a single message or grand takeaway. Please accept these pages as my story, perhaps a different kind of tale.

To preserve the privacy of certain parties and to present a compelling story, there have been alterations and adjustments throughout this narrative. Nevertheless, I try to stay true to my own perceptions and experiences during the time frame of the memoir.

The views expressed in this publication are my own and do not necessarily reflect the opinions or policies of my current employer or other professional affiliations.

My invitation is for you to stay creative in your own career planning, to allow yourself to think outside the box, and to carry passion with you wherever your righteous path may take you. I write this with the deepest respect for my family, friends, colleagues, teachers, mentors, mentees, clients, writers, editors, and my publishing team.

CHAPTER ONE
Starting A Journey

At several points in my career as a doctor, I have considered stepping out of the field of medicine. This is probably not unusual. In fact, I would imagine that thinking about career change is quite common, especially for people like doctors in high stress professions with the potential for burnout, though I have yet to locate a comprehensive quantitative research study on the matter. As one of my colleagues wisely remarked, "Everyone has a story." You could say that this is mine.

I am not so adventurous as to abandon the field of medicine in the way of fictional characters or to relocate to some exotic island. For me, the sensible, middle path has always been optimal. And yet, at times I have felt compelled to carve out a comfortable niche independent of medicine in order to preserve my identity–baffling, considering how hard one works to get accepted into medical school.

Reflecting on your career is a necessary and healthy part of being a professional. It can mean anything from staying the course, volunteering, joining a new organization, or even discarding your day job in pursuit of something entirely new. For me, my career has episodically meant envisioning professional ventures outside the field of medicine, like feature writing, event planning, and international hospitality.

Most people would label this as mere daydreaming and toss it off as trivial, certainly not noteworthy. But I confess that at particularly challenging moments in my psychiatric career these meanderings could get pretty intense, like the time very early on that I was almost assaulted by an agitated patient and fortunately managed to escape the consulting room just in time to call for security assistance.

On that occasion, as I walked down the hall away from the sounds and clamor of an emergency intervention, I questioned what I was doing in a field where a major goal seemed to be to avoid injury, let alone one's own demise. That day was pretty shaky, and I felt relatively conflicted about continuing in psychiatry. Under the circumstances, who wouldn't have felt that way?

And yet, I love being a physician and am proud of all that's involved in patient care. Truthfully, the pull of having my own side business or creative project has kept me energized. You could say that the analytic and creative sides, as for many others, work in tandem, and work hard!

Many people come from family backgrounds like mine: middle class, financially comfortable, and achievement oriented. They undoubtedly have interesting stories to share about their own career paths. Perhaps they, like me, received a subliminal message to pursue something their parents deemed worthy, which, for my parents, probably meant education, law, or social service—certainly never medicine—at least not for their daughter at that point, and not right at the beginning . . .

We lived in a leafy suburb on the edge of Boston, replete with stately homes and craggy oak trees standing tall after decades of battling the nor'easters.

Nobody in Boston cared about their lawns or the intricate landscaping of their shrubbery. Instead most opted for the casual, weekend putter around their backyard to adjust the rose beds. You never saw a *Keep off—pesticide treated area!* warning painted on a two-by-four sign stuck between overgrown blades on a patchy lawn.

I imagine that for many Bostonians, the priority was to accumulate as many academic honors as possible rather than to have the perfect front yard, and, frankly, I could never quite figure out my position in all of this academic snobbery.

We were within walking distance of downtown, a bonus for all of my planned social adventures and exploration of the city's happenings. One temperate summer day, at the age of sixteen, I decided to walk into downtown Boston by myself. Usually, I took this walk with one or two friends, but on this particular day, it being mid-summer, most of my friends were away.

First, I stopped in Copley Square for a takeout lunch, devouring two spinach croissants, downed with chilled, tart cranberry juice. Then I strolled down Commonwealth Avenue, eventually landing on the Boston Commons, pausing for ten minutes on the Boston Public Garden footbridge to take in the Swan Boats and lush flower beds.

Parked out on one of the Common's gentler slopes, the one that spills onto Charles Street, was my high school buddy, Rafe. Over the summer, his sandy brown locks had collected into soft curls around his neck, and he was sporting gold Aviator-style wire-rim glasses, different from the square brown ones he'd worn at school. I did a double take, not initially recognizing him. Rafe looked tanned and prosperous in contrast to his habitual, pale, winter aura.

"Rafe, great to see you! How's your summer going? What are you up to?" Rafe was seated in one of two lawn chairs angled at forty-five degrees. Both chairs were positioned in front of a canvas pup tent overflowing with what appeared to be invoice materials plus stacks of secondhand books. A sign was propped up between the chairs.

"Hey Jane! Really nice to see you too! I'm making a living, of course." He then gestured down and to the left. "Catch my sign. This sure beats waiting tables." I glanced down at the "infamous" sign:

FOR FIVE DOLLARS
I will argue with you about anything for 15 minutes. And I will take either side. Rafael.

"Good God, Rafe, this is outrageous! Too much. Love it! Just love it! Very intriguing. How did you come up with this idea?" I had to bend forward and use the hem of my skirt to wipe away my laughter tears. My classmates had all known that Rafe was brilliant, maybe even eccentric, but this edgy? Rafe continued in his slightly husky, boyish voice, "The arguing booth has been an incredibly lucrative gig. You have no idea how many people signed up today. Tons. Plus, there are the tips. And if the 'argument' exceeds fifteen minutes, they get charged an extra five. They don't mind. I don't know, I guess people are lonely and game for a sounding board."

"Usually, we discuss politics, but yeah . . . this one guy showed up in a business suit and wanted to review the pros and cons of 'filing for a divorce' from his Skye Terrier who evidently has become a royal pain in the ass. You know, putting the dog up for adoption, not down, for Christ's sake. Whatever . . . I don't really give a damn as long as they pay me." Rafe smiled.

"Hmm . . . well, good luck. Hope you can sell off some of the book collection." I pointed to the pile of books jammed into the tent. "See ya. Keep me posted on your summer and stay safe," my parting words as I tilted my head to one side and continued my outing, for some reason apprehensive about his security.

As a teenager filled with the belief that details somehow got magically worked out, I did not ponder what time Rafe would close up shop that day, where he would dine that night, or how he would manage transporting his abundant work materials back and forth to his parents' home. Those were the kind of details more characteristic of my parents' adult mindset.

Like any other major city, Boston had its fair share of crime, but shootings and stabbings in broad daylight? Unheard of, particularly in those little foothills of Beacon Hill. You could sit for hours on the Boston Commons and feel reasonably safe commiserating with other souls planted on the lawn.

After college, Rafe went on to become a successful screenwriter and entrepreneur. Why am I telling you this? Perhaps Rafe's avant-garde enterprise, at the time a source of both amusement and reverence among my high school buddies, ingrained within me an entrepreneurial spirit, to follow my own inspirational path and simultaneously expect to be paid in the process.

My parents were hardworking educators, my mother a grade-school teacher and my father a graphic artist and art historian. But when it came to career advice, they were curiously noninterventional.

I was never certain of what they expected for me career wise, but I understood that the bar was set high based on their tony cultural tastes: theater, symphony, foreign films, fundraisers, dinner parties, and gallery openings, to name a few. It seemed that they were always out, painting the town. If they were alive today, they would undoubtedly object to this portrayal, as they considered themselves to be highly attentive to their children's needs while also managing their own life and identity separate from parenthood. You had to admire them for their enlightened brand of antihelicopter parenting.

I have heard my peers describe that from day one of preschool through the college graduation ceremony, they were primed to be doctors. Perhaps their parents happened to be doctors and wished for their children to join the family tradition. Or, if they were of the first generation, maybe they were held to the expectation of making their family proud, wearing the banner of the American dream.

That was not my circumstance. My first-generation American parents raised my brother and I during the 1970s, against a backdrop of what some now label good old-fashioned American liberalism. I cannot remember who it was, my mother or my father, but one of them literally said during dinner, "Listen, if you want to become a garbage collector, and that's what would make you happy, then go for it. Fine by us." Presumably they were giving an egalitarian nod to those working outside of an academic bubble and affirming confidence in their daughter's ability to make her own decisions. I have the feeling that some of my friends may have encountered similar faux inducements from their parents, as verbal laissez-faire was the politically correct parenting style throughout the seventies.

I have reluctantly come to realize that the lure of medicine was a decision, not a calling. "A calling" implies a dedication so intense and comprehensive that personal needs become subsumed under a higher purpose. There are probably colleagues of mine so committed to the delivery of health care that they appear to be linked to their answering systems twenty-four-seven—during lunches, parties, and even college tours with their kids. I recall one poor father, most likely in health care, on his cell phone during an entire college tour, presumably talking a patient through a crisis while his son, along with my daughter, was absorbing the scenic campus surroundings and jesting with the student guide.

When starting a new practice, the doctor may carry a reluctance about training their patients to wait for a return call within a reasonable time frame as opposed to responding right away. While that degree of caution should be respected, it is potentially unsustainable over one's long-term career. Being caring and dedicated also requires professional boundaries.

With deference to my parents' progressive values, for me, the study of medicine was a process that could make a positive social impact, and also ensured prestige and financial security, as I vowed never to ask my parents for one dime upon completing my education.

Upon discovering that I was considering a career in psychiatry, my father, Roy, pushed back. "You're not really going into that bullshit!" he exclaimed. Dad was a World War II veteran who held strong beliefs about the importance of community service way before "community service" became a popular catchphrase.

My father was not shy about expressing his views, now that I was considering a relatively concrete course of study, and as the saying goes, he did not suffer fools gladly. He plunged right in. "I see you in primary care working with families to bring about systemic change, maybe even in pediatrics, but not walled away in some insulated office, listening to people indulge in the painstaking process of superfluous contemplation. People are not always going to be happy. That's life. Besides, what's the point of all that medical training? Janey, please. I beg you, reflect and reconsider!"

I adored my father, wanting nothing more than to please him. He was soft-spoken, yet powerful and effective as a leader, always the consummate diplomat except apparently now with his daughter. I felt my throat tighten as if I was a little girl primed for scolding. I recognized being too emotional in the moment to proceed further in discussion while appreciating that he respected me enough to be candid in his opinion. And thus, in silence, I nodded.

My mother just stood there, interpreted to mean that she held no particular opinion on the matter. That was unusual for Mom, who like my father, held fast to her opinions, and like my father, had a strong but more extroverted presence.

Mostly, I felt shame over disappointing Dad. But in the back of my mind was the unsettling realization that my generation would evolve beyond the encased, post–World War II world of my parents, a world defined by clear moral standards, right versus wrong, liberal versus reactionary, a world that would become more ambiguous as time marched on.

Later, when I became a full-fledged psychiatric resident, my father would periodically inquire about updates in the field of brain research, trying to find ways to stay connected with me through my training experience, which, ironically, I experienced as a poignant effort on his part to apologize.

In contrast to today's practice climate, that was an era when psychiatrists could actually make a decent living. You set a consulting fee, you saw the patient, you handed them a bill, and voilà, you were handsomely paid.

Since the 1980s, earning capacity for psychiatrists has gradually diminished with the establishment of managed care, a complicated system whereby insurance companies set out to tame spiraling medical costs by regulating participating doctors' fees as well as the number of allowable yearly visits. Subsequently, there evolved the resource-based relative value scale, the standardization of doctors' fees, implemented by the Centers of Medicare & Medicaid Services (CMS).

Once the federal government stepped in to standardize physician reimbursement, private carriers followed suit, placing further limits on physician fees in accordance with Medicare. Any doctor participating with an insurance panel as either an in-network or out-of-network provider could expect to write off a sizable portion of their customary charges.

This still holds true today—take a glance at an explanation of benefits (EOB) rendered by the medical insurance company to both you and your physician. It will show staggering write-offs. Hypothetically, if your doctor's customary charge for a medication visit and lab work is $350, the commercial insurance carrier may elect to write off 40 percent of the doctor's customary charge. Subtract from that the patient's cost sharing amount (e.g. the patient's co-pay due at the time of the visit), say $20. The physician is then left with a net insurance payout of $190. Who can make a comfortable living writing off almost 50 percent for every service rendered?[1]

In 2013, the median salary for a psychiatrist was reported as $188,000, as opposed to $313,000 for a surgeon.[2] Sixty-seven percent of those surveyed additionally reported that, as of 2019, within the preceding five years they had either held steady in earnings or were actually losing income. The driving factors for the decline in revenue were a higher administrative burden, declining insurance reimbursements, mounting overhead costs, difficulty collecting from patients, and the need to invest in rapidly expanding technology.[3]

Financial state of my medical practice one year ago:

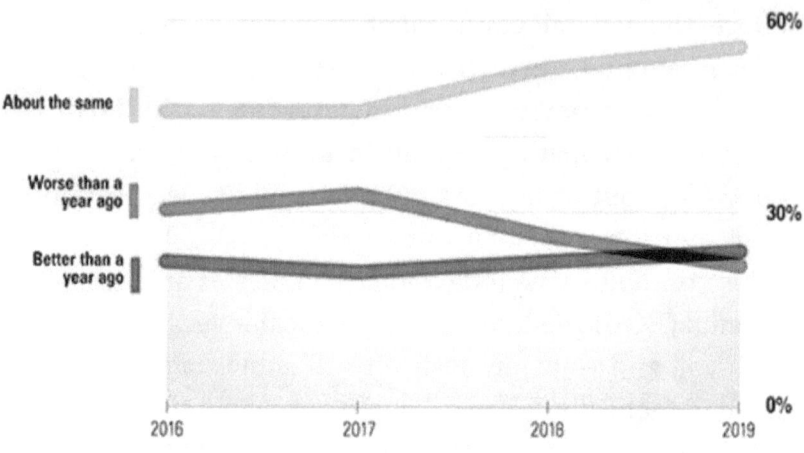

Financial state of my medical practice five years ago:

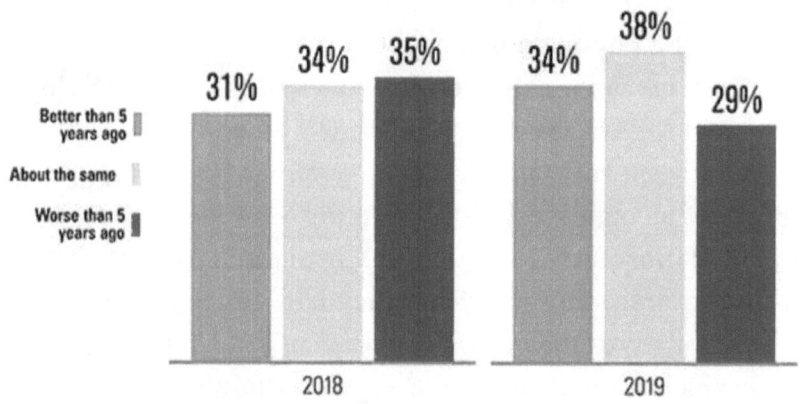

These figures originally appeared in Medical Economics, 2020;97(9) and have been reproduced by Psychiatric Times with permission.

Dr. Catherine Heffner, a valued medical colleague, related that she wanted to be a psychiatrist her whole life, enduring many hardships, setbacks, and academic challenges in order to secure her current position as a lucrative and successful private physician. "Now we have to see so many clients to make a decent salary—nobody wins with this formula. Doctors have become more defensive, frenzied, harried, and reluctant. Now that we have this new vocabulary word, *burnout*, we have to replete all of the depletion," describing her experience in private practice.

My end-of-the-summer teenage mindset was oblivious to the financial challenges of the medical industry. I mapped out a road to independence and prosperity one luxurious August afternoon while reposing next to a trellis of roses climbing up the side of our home. I had no idea what lay ahead in terms of the time commitment, lifestyle sacrifice, and the eventual reduced earning power of physicians. After all, what could any seventeen-year-old have been expected to know about the medical minefields that lay ahead?

Later, at a campus cocktail hour as a sophomore at Smith College, I met my first bona fide physician role model, a primary care physician and fellow Smith graduate who unintentionally influenced me to pursue medicine. We were at an outdoor meet and greet on the college president's lawn one Saturday afternoon. The physician was receiving a distinguished alumna award. The weather was crisp, the sky cloudless, and it was the kind of autumn day when you are filled with optimism, ready to tackle all the roadblocks lying in your path. My parents were there, and we all had imbibed one or two glasses of white wine.

The doctor presented as self-assured, stoic, and quite different from most other women I had encountered. She had a remarkably commanding presence, which struck me as very impactful given that she was on a career path still somewhat uncommon for women. It wasn't so much her acceptance speech as her supremely confident manner that impressed me.

After the award ceremony, I approached her and shared that I had started taking premed courses and hoped to apply to medical school. Truthfully, I was harboring second thoughts about the tremendous level of intensity involved in being a premed student, not to mention the ensuing responsibility of being a physician, but she did not have to know that.

"What is your life like as a doctor?" I posed.

She paused for a moment. "It's a long haul. It's a ton of work. You have to really know if you are up for it with all your heart and soul. Think it through carefully." Absent was the proclamation: "Isn't that wonderful! Your parents must be so proud of you!" The doctor's cautionary reply went over my head in the buzz of the chardonnay, the glow of the party, and the security of having my parents right there beside me.

Buoyed up by the nurturing environment of Smith College, I eventually arrived on the Manhattan scene to begin medical school. One look at the imposing architecture of the old Bellevue Hospital sprawling along the East River sent shivers down my spine, filling me with dread, trepidation, and doubt. What was I thinking, training as a physician in this massive medical complex steeped in history? And that is where the rest of my narration into the field of psychiatry and then onto the world of beauty begins.

The historic facade of Bellevue Hospital, New York City

CHAPTER TWO
Training to Become a Doctor

I am a psychiatrist. In the morning, I must occasionally remind myself of this fact, as my self-perception generally revolves around just trying to be a responsible person in this increasingly digital, entropic universe. And yet I am privileged to share the same professional stage with some of the notables: Drs. Sigmund Freud, Frieda Fromm-Reichman, and Chester M. Pierce, to name a few, plus any number of sharp colleagues and professors who have served as my teachers.[4]

Dr. Naomi Weinshenker, like Dr. Heffner, is a respected psychiatrist in solo practice and encounters an astounding number of people who have no idea what the difference is between psychiatrists and psychologists is. She believes that it may be a matter of mistaken vocabulary rather than mistaken identity—they likely know the difference between the two disciplines, but not totally. Thus, Dr. Weinshenker lets the matter slip, in the interest of smooth conversation.

What Dr. Weinshenker may not choose to explore in the moment is that the difference lies in the training, four years of medical or osteopathic school, followed by a four-year postgraduate residency for psychiatrists versus a generally six-year prepatory program for psychologists. That amounts to a two-year training differential that must be considered when it comes to a comprehensive understanding of how psychiatric medications work in the human body.

That is not to minimize the rigorous postgraduate training that psychologists must undergo to become the highly skilled professionals that they are in conducting psychotherapy, cognitive/behavioral treatments, and neurobehavioral evaluations. But theoretically, until 2002, when New Mexico was the first of five states to legally grant psychologists prescribing privileges, only psychiatrists, along with other physicians, could prescribe the psychotropic medications that regulate the mind.[5]

From the standpoint of safe prescribing, a residency in psychiatry that encompasses twelve core competencies places the psychiatrist at a distinct advantage over psychologists who, in certain states, may choose to tack on to their PhD degree a relatively brief prescribing certification course so that they, like psychiatrists, can legally prescribe medication (Table 1).

The psychiatric residency training at Bellevue Hospital was, as expected, more intense than my previous exposure to psychiatry as a New York University medical student during the one or two-month behavioral health rotation. In addition to mastering all the academic rigor as outlined in Table 1, the psychiatry resident was unintentionally the keeper of the guard—the grand, romanticized version of mental illness in America, symbolized by the very edifice of old Bellevue Hospital.

After all, the term *Bellevue* is a household word and has become irreparably intertwined with the state of being crazy in places far off the grid from New York City, not to mention the hospital's numerous guest appearances in fictional works, nonfictional accounts, and media productions.[6]

A portion of the original red brick building was dedicated to the psychiatry residency, no longer the case today, as the training program has shifted to a different locale within the hospital complex. After walking down a narrow side street, windswept by the East River in the dead of winter, you arrived inside the facility through massive stone pillars each separated by wrought iron.

This entrance is presumably featured in the movie *Zelig*, where actress Mia Farrow, portraying psychiatrist Dr. Eudora Fletcher, paces back and forth through the iconic entryway, deeply reflective on the treatment of her patient, Zelig.[7]

House staff were given old-fashioned keys to open the doors. Today, those keys would amount to a collector's item based on more technically sophisticated means of entry and exit.

Upon entering the building, you maintained a heightened vigilance, a preparedness for God knows what. For me, there was an internalized sense that absolutely anything could happen within those walls, though in reality I am unaware that anything major did happen. Maybe it was just my own prejudice, perhaps an unjustified premonition on my part, as the wards and offices were all highly secured.

Except, an additional feature, often overlooked, was the pesky rodent population. Those particular mice were not as inconspicuous as they believed themselves to be. One day, I was interviewing a patient pulled off the streets by the police. A mouse steadily inched its way from the corner of the office to the tip of my shoe. My patient took a breather from her disorganized, psychotic, ramble, and in the most considerate manner leaned over and patted my knee. "Listen doctor, I can see that you are getting upset about the mouse. Why don't we take a break and reconvene later when you are feeling better."

On another occasion, I was paged to one of the units in the early evening. For that particular unit, you had to wait outside the doors for security clearance. It was summer, and I happened to be wearing open-toed clogs, in fashion at the time. All of a sudden, something smallish and furry seemed to settle on top of my foot. My first instinct was to doubt my perception, as I could

Table 1: Areas of core competence during psychiatric residency

Making a psychiatric diagnosis and dynamic formulation through the psychiatric interview
Studying the pathology of the human personality
Reviewing brain and central nervous system anatomy and physiology
Studying the major mental disorders including symptoms, etiology, treatment, and psychosocial factors
Being aware of the mind/body interplay, how physical disease impacts mental health and the converse
Learning the repertoire of treatment modalities and psychotropic medications- mechanisms of action, indication, side effects, genetic metabolism, and drug-drug interactions
Understanding the treatment of substance and alcohol use disorders
Reviewing the human life cycle including developmental milestones
Exploring alternative treatment options such as trans-magnetic cranial stimulation and electroconvulsive therapy
Understanding facilitators of and barriers to behavioral health care including sociodemographic disparities
Being introduced to the tenets of psychoanalysis and psychotherapy
Integrating behavioral health and economic models into clinical practice

not believe that any critter in Manhattan or elsewhere would have such colossal audacity.

Imagine! After all, is it not understood that the mouse is more afraid of the human than the other way around? Glancing down, there was a gray visitor with its slimy tail positioned in the center of my left foot. I proceeded to let out the most blood curdling scream ever to grace those halls. The hospital security guard quickly appeared and, judging from his bemused smile, determined that I was safe but greatly flustered. He was probably used to mice, but not necessarily psychiatric residents who were that upset. At least it wasn't a rat—that would've induced a syncopal episode.

The institution of Bellevue served as a reminder that you were working toward the higher purpose of treating severe mental illness, transcending the daily, personal hassles, like misplacing your checkbook or figuring out how in God's name you were going to deal with a rent increase, a common occurrence in Manhattan.

Not to sound maudlin, but in between the daily grind and at the most unexpected moments you could be filled with a surge of purpose almost bordering on a spiritual experience. Maybe you noticed a storied aspect to the windows, now sealed and grimy, evoking a sense of history in their grandeur and intricately molded frames. Or, if you were fortunate to be assigned to an office facing the southeast, you might catch the sunlight fluttering in from Queens, over the East River, and through the streaky plate glass window overhanging your desk.

Or you could find that same hopeful internal stirring during the weekly case conference as your mentors effortlessly unraveled the intricacies of a particularly difficult patient. It never ceased to amaze me how faculty members could sit down with the most tragically damaged patient and reconstruct an entirely coherent, clinical history including subtle points you may have missed with access only to the patient interview and the most basic of corroborative data.

Residents would typically save the most challenging cases for these conferences. As if watching a play or a chess match, the psychiatry professor, clearly seasoned in interviewing techniques, would open with the perfect remark in order to unlock the clinical puzzle. A few masterful, well-timed questions and pauses could peel back layers of obscurity to form an alliance with the healthy and narrative part of the patient's psyche, the part that remembered the street where they grew up, their parent's names, something nice that happened during their childhood, and how they came to be hospitalized in the first place.

While you attended these conferences, you suspended the world of the mundane, your task lists, your incomplete reports, and numerous phone calls awaiting a reply. For that one cherished hour, you sat back in awe and drew in the otherworldly essence of why you chose to become a psychiatrist.

I cannot overstate how much I relied on my coresidents to get through the training. The residency program was a tight-knit and supportive community that, for me, functioned as life support. There was an unspoken bond of support and unconditional acceptance. You were there with your colleagues, and like them, putting in long hours to tend to the medical needs of patients. You and your coresidents had survived the ordeal of medical school, and somehow now there was less to prove. The residency was also a gateway to building professional confidence and a path for future career opportunities in clinical care and scientific research.

Obviously, you did not have control over every aspect of your cases. For example, your patient might decline medication, threaten to sign out, or require commitment to a longer-term care facility. Social service agencies were hovering, constantly requesting information and documentation in a way that at times, as much as you hated to admit it, felt intrusive to your workflow.

But that was par for the course, integral to your training, and you had to logically accept that many of your patients relied on their disability payments, the welfare system, public shelters, and community kitchens. Afterall, Bellevue was a city hospital, known for servicing all who walked through its doors. There was also the view that once you emerged from the Bellevue training, you could probably handle anything. The residency had overprepared you for your next clinical assignment and, figuratively speaking, your life.

A conversation with Dr. Anthony Grieco, Associate Dean of New York University Medical School, an esteemed mentor, confirmed my perception of the value of the training experience. Dr. Grieco believes that "Bellevue Hospital is unique in putting the student front and center in the patient's management, and the patient is appreciative. The educational benefit is that recent graduates are ahead of the curve . . . . They are well prepared and confident. In addition, they become skilled in the art as well as science of medicine which these days often involves analyzing reams of data generated by technology in search of what is relevant."

People think that in comparison to other medical specialties, training to be a psychiatrist is easy. In fact, medical students may select psychiatry as the least rigorous option or the softer specialty. At least, that used to be the train of thought.

Remember the classic treatise, *The House of God*, so popular in the late 1970s that it almost became "mandatory" reading for house staff across the country? At the end of an exceptionally traumatic year as a medical intern in a large teaching hospital, the fictional protagonist, Dr. Roy Basch, throws in the towel and opts to become a shrink. The reader understands that Dr. Basch simply can't take it any longer—the pressure, the workplace chaos, and the sobering realization that despite all of the team's best efforts, the patient may die.[8]

I confess that those were my sentiments, that psychiatry would be more manageable when I applied to stay on as a psychiatric resident at New York University at the completion of medical school. While I had internalized my father's plea to enter the specialty of primary care, the lighter call requirement for psychiatry was too enticing to pass up, every fourth as opposed to every third night. That amounted to one extra night of sleep per week and plausibly four to five extra nights of sleep per month, depending on whether it was leap year.

Plus, you got paid to read, in this instance, to intellectually digest the highlights of character disorders and psychoanalytic theory. For me, Wilhelm Reich's theory of the human personality was especially compelling until the ill-fated doctor veered off into a direction that landed him in legal difficulties.[9] Moreover, the less onerous call schedule would open the possibility of a personal life provided you could stay awake.

Nothing in this train of thinking could have been further from the truth. There were on-call nights during the second year of training when the psychiatry resident assigned to cover the emergency room could evaluate multiple patients, back-to-back, many of whom were intoxicated or cognitively compromised. A substantial number of the emergency room patients were brought in from the street by the police and presented as confused, agitated, or somnolent, certainly not verbally cooperative for an initial screening interview.

Because of the difficulty in being able to get a comprehensive understanding of the patient's needs at the time of initial presentation, the second-year resident was permitted to defer making a final disposition until the patient could be reevaluated, which for me, was the following morning with my chief resident.

Alec was the chief resident assigned to supervise me for the year. We would routinely meet the morning right after the call in an office off to the side of the psychiatry emergency room. Alec was punctual and never forgot to bring both of us hot coffee and fresh bagels for our "Monday morning quarterback" breakfast. When he appeared, typically dressed in a tweed sports jacket with a coordinated maroon print tie, I felt utterly relieved to see him, as his entrance signified that, thank God, my on-call shift was almost over.

Alec was a superb teacher and supportive of my clinical judgment. He was interested in understanding the thought processes that went into his supervisees' decisions. The supervisee was not expected to be medically omniscient, nor to have memorized the entire compendium of emergency room psychiatry. In many instances, Alec and I would return to a patient's bedside to conduct a joint interview, often with more success during the second go around as the patient invariably understood the pecking order, that they needed to be cooperative now that the chief was present.

Alec and I would then review toxicology screens, blood alcohol levels, x-rays, and whatever other pertinent data had trickled in overnight, plus the corroborative history obtained from community sources and available family members, finally arriving at the ultimate clinical objective, whether to admit or discharge the patient from the hospital.

As you might expect, the final disposition was not always straightforward or welcomed. You could get caught up in the crossfire of family dynamics—whether hospitalization was viewed by relatives as either a mark of shame or, conversely, a gesture of salvation. Generally, there was no in-between. Families often pleaded their case to have their loved one admitted, sharing with you all the troubling behaviors that may not have been forthcoming during the evaluation, often related to the covert use of substance and skillfully omitted by the patient during the interview. Those were situations where Alex was a godsend, invaluable as a supervisor, reasoning through and supporting the trainee's judgment.

I confess to profound exhaustion by the end of those mornings, having no idea how to make it through the rest of a tightly scheduled day. It is also fair to mention that my wrinkled, coffee-stained, white medical jacket and deep undereye circles, in contrast to Alec's ever-pressed professional look, were, for me, highly problematic.

Even comparing myself to Alec, now a chief resident, well past the obligatory all-night, rite of passage duty, was clearly not rational. But in all fairness your mind works like this on twenty-four hours of sleep deprivation; the less the sleep, the less the censoring of random thoughts.

Funny to consider that in the midst of this intense training program, the sense of accomplishment derived from surviving those brutal on-call shifts could be possibly eclipsed by the triviality of one's crumpled coat. Undoubtedly some of my colleagues felt the opposite, looking like a train wreck at the end of a difficult call was a badge of honor.

Bellevue lay across town from Manhattan's fashion district, not that the latter neighborhood, famous for its cutting-edge glamour, had any more than a fleeting influence on my sense of style. But just knowing that particular block of streets was in close proximity served as a reminder that elegance counted for something, my wardrobe playing a strong supporting role in staying creative and humanized during the residency.

As a young professional woman, I aspired to project myself as effortlessly assembled—a touch of exotic jewelry around the neck and tastefully applied brown lipstick completing my version of the Boston-Manhattan sophisticate—never corporate and slightly offbeat. In retrospect, for a second-year resident to look fabulous the day after taking a call was an exercise in futility.

I would periodically take advantage of New York University's offer of free theater tickets, just to get my mind off major mental illness and the filing of documents, at least for an hour. The medical school was directly across the street from the psychiatric hospital. There in the medical school you could find two long perpendicular corridors with mellow lighting and a serene atmosphere.

At the corner where the hallways converged, past the photographs honoring distinguished Bellevue faculty, and on a narrow wall, you would encounter a glass-encased listing of all the current Broadway and off-Broadway shows, plus the happenings at Lincoln Center with available restaurant and theater packages. The university was extremely generous in providing discount tickets that you could select from this list.

I would study the list for a while, planning my next night out on the town, what show to see, whom to invite, and where to dine. If a colleague happened to appear alongside me, also to presumably scan the city's happenings, there was an unwritten rule of conduct that neither of us spoke one word while weighing in on such vital decisions. "List review" was taken very seriously at New York University, the code of silence at the glass case perhaps as important as the quiet atmosphere of an exam room.

In fact, that little spot was my idea of heaven. I simply adored it! It was so civilized, and it was there that the mindset to stay connected to a world bigger than my immediate Bellevue psychiatric world gained a foothold.

CHAPTER THREE
Setting Up a Practice

During the third year of psychiatry training, every Bellevue resident was required to rotate through the outpatient department and develop their own caseload of patients. One day, a young adult patient who was assigned to my psychotherapy roster and with whom I would meet on a weekly basis randomly commented, "Dr. Sofair, I see you setting up a private practice when you are done with me." She added, "You should do that." Her choice of words, *when you are done with me*, was telling. We exchanged five minutes of weighty, but polite silence. I was uncertain as to whether to make an interpretation or just accept her observation at face value and keep the session moving.

Still a rookie, I decided on the latter—to keep the conversation flowing rather than run the risk of making a potentially intrusive interpretation about her fears of abandonment and have her bolt from treatment in a halo of shame.

Yes, that can happen in the field of psychiatry! As a beginner, you, the doctor, are intellectually excited about the study of human psychopathology and believe you may know more about the patient's inner workings than does the patient. Typically, the patient will push back in a variety of ways, including, at one extreme, finding a new doctor, the ultimate failing report card. Over time, you learn from this experience and become more circumspect in making therapeutic interventions.

Nevertheless, my patient's remarks resonated and endured. Despite having reassured my patient that I was there for her, and that the future lay open for both of us, I did move on as did she. Upon completing the residency, and after several frenzied hospital positions, I set up my own private practice.

Private practice is not for everyone. Some physicians may justifiably prefer the structure and security of a hospital position. Among the many perks of working within a hospital or healthcare network are a low overhead, a built-in case load, institutionally provided professional insurance, ready access to consultation with your community of colleagues, teaching opportunities, and the potential for managerial and academic growth.

Yet private practice is for those who need control over where they work, the hours they work, whom they treat, whom they decline to treat, and which colleagues with whom they choose to interact. Psychiatrists before me have certainly written numerous articles about how to set up your own practice. As with starting any business, taking the dive into the uncertainty of the private practice world can be daunting.

The devil is in the details. Finding affordable consulting space, establishing a communication system with your patients, hiring and retaining valued administrative staff, registering your practice with the requisite regulatory agencies, joining a voluntary hospital staff, obtaining professional risk insurance, determining how best to collect fees, and engaging and keeping your referrals are all important things to keep in mind for a psychiatrist. These are some of the many items that wondrously appear on your to-do list once you, the recently graduated resident, transition into "true physician adulthood."

There is no question that building a patient roster remains

front and center for any private practitioner when starting out, as was the case for me. At the beginning, the number of referrals you received symbolized your worth as a doctor. With six patients on the schedule, if three either canceled or missed their appointment, it was unbelievably disheartening. You began to doubt your decision of having left the security of being a hospital employee. Among other worries, how were you going to make the month's overhead?

Every physician knows these risks and probably has their own private saga of practice challenges. But we all have to start somewhere. A doctor is as good as their most recent session, akin to the restaurant business—if the last served meal was mediocre, then the owner may as well kiss that customer goodbye.

Loyalty for the private psychiatrist, really any psychiatrist, can be equally ephemeral, like a burst of sunlight amid an ominous, stormy summer sky. Based on my experience, the reasons for cancellations and broken appointments were never clear, at least for 50 percent of the patients, but obviously there was a subjective and nonmeasurable factor at bay.

In the interest of self-protection, I opted to avoid digging deeper, perhaps less intrepid than my colleagues who had to get the gory details of why the patient left, or what the patient honestly thought about their initial sessions with the doctor. For me, however, ignorance was bliss. This preceded the patient satisfaction surveys that emerged with the trend toward consumerism in healthcare.

Early on, the luxury of screening patients for "the perfect fit" was not there, as I needed to stack my calendar with appointments and build rapport with valued referral sources. I cannot begin to recount the many patients accepted into the practice who, in retrospect, were not the best fit. Some patients were looking for more research-oriented specialists who would run a gamut of laboratory panels to pinpoint their exact mental condition. They may have become frustrated to learn that psychiatry did not have the repertoire of laboratory and diagnostic tools concomitant with the other medical specialties.

Take vitamin D, for example. A commonly seen low vitamin D level is neither necessary nor sufficient to make a diagnosis of major depression. And yet, sometimes patients would request a vitamin panel despite the lack of clearcut supporting science. When someone is suffering from debilitating depression, they are looking for every potential clinical solution.

You quickly learned that without the proper screening and case selection, your work-life boundaries could become tenuous. There was a risk of being flooded with phone calls, not to mention cumulative administrative details seven days per week.

An interesting keyword in clinical management is *urgent*. Is what the patient may consider *urgent* truly urgent, or can the matter be safely deferred until the next business day? As I have alluded, this is an issue with which each doctor must grapple. While you never want to miss a genuine emergency, I have come to believe that there is no uniform consensus among my private practice colleagues as to how available you are expected to be after regular business hours.

Emergency calls would typically flow in via telephone, the hospital pager, and later through an email system. Holidays could be challenging as patients would feel their most vulnerable and panicky facing too much down time with family around. And that is when they were invariably hurting the most and needed to have an appointment.

My first consulting space was idyllic, located in a beautiful Victorian home on a tree-lined formerly residential street and not far from the center of town. I felt privileged to be invited to rent space in that practice, working alongside reputable and trustworthy colleagues and was excited to begin this new chapter.

I sat behind a large desk, with the patient facing me on

the opposite side. In one corner of the room, a nonworking fireplace was covered by an old-fashioned iron grate. Adjacent to the fireplace were two large sealed French windows looking out onto a wrap-around porch. The room was wall-papered in a warm ivory pattern, with a belle epoque sofa stationed in front of the sealed French windows, and tasteful carpet gracing the floor.

What could go wrong in this beautiful space? Administratively speaking, plenty! The day could run away from you on the flip of a coin, the countless schedule adjustments, pharmacy refill requests, insurance requests, not to mention tightly booked appointments with the waiting room picking up.

An issue that became more pressing than enjoying my office space was the handling of rapidly changing technology and administrative demands, to ensure smooth insurance coverage of treatment and medication and ultimately to earn a steady income. I began to feel pressured by treatment and medication authorizations, and it became abundantly clear that the office could simply not run without a knowledgeable office coordinator.

I had never hired an office administrator, let alone as a solo physician on a fixed budget. Plus, I had to make certain that whoever came on board had a soothing, professional manner, worked well with the patients, and was most discrete.

In the end, I went through a series of office administrators before hiring a talented individual with an extensive background in healthcare, coding, and billing. She and I navigated much transition and uncertainty, later intensified during the pandemic when we once again teamed up upon my return to New Jersey and after my two-year hiatus working in Connecticut. It was a heartbreak when she decided to step down to allow for more family time.

Adapting my practice to the digital world—a project in of itself—was only partially achieved in the setting up of an electronic prescribing system. A full electronic medical record remained for me a work-in-progress during my entire tenure in solo practice. For the solo practitioner, to implement a full electronic medical record is time-consuming and costly. Several of my colleagues worked with software engineers to custom design their own systems. I did my due diligence, of course, researching the various electronic medical records on the market available for psychiatry, ranging from the rudimentary to the more elaborate, but nothing ever quite gelled.

A fully appointed digital program should be able to replicate the workflow of your office: record clinical notes, schedule appointments, generate patient invoices, collect and organize revenue, send prescriptions directly to pharmacies, import collateral documents, organize and interpret lab results, and, in essence, virtually operationalize the entire practice on a secure computer.

One prospective electronic medical record required that I fly down to the Ozark region for a weekend training seminar. That particular system proved to have hardware requirements too sophisticated for my computer, only to be discovered upon returning to New Jersey.

CHAPTER FOUR
Entertaining Change

One summer weekend, about a year into the practice, my husband and I trekked up to Cooperstown, New York for a getaway. We had tickets to attend the Glimmerglass Festival, planned to visit the National Baseball Hall of Fame, and had booked ourselves into a charming bed-and-breakfast.

By now, I was entertaining passing thoughts of opening and running a bed-and-breakfast with the belief that running a small inn would be a piece of cake—pun intended—in comparison to managing a medical practice. That was my tendency; when the field of psychiatry—or anything else for that matter—became too challenging, I would consider a plan B. I believe having a backup plan is a fairly typical coping mechanism.

The inn was run by a husband-and-wife team estimated to be somewhere in their middle years. Every afternoon at 4 o'clock they held a poetry reading accompanied by freshly brewed tea, homemade scones, a fruit and cheese board, and wine flights. In other words, the gourmet works! On arrival day, we missed the reading which overlapped with our concert plans, but the following morning, at breakfast, we had the opportunity to chat with the co-owners.

"I am sorry you missed our poetry reading last night. It

was really spot-on, very special—a local poet who writes on the variations and spiritual aspects of nature," explained Martin, a kind and intelligent man who approached our table. "Perhaps you can join us for this afternoon's reading, this time total stream of consciousness, pretty wacky stuff. Incidentally, may I inquire where you are from and how you found our inn?"

For a soft-spoken, retiring man, Martin wasn't doing too badly doubling as a salesman, event promoter, and investigator of his guest's personal details.

My husband, who prefers watching ESPN to a poetry reading any day, could barely camouflage an eye roll, politely explaining how we had researched Martin and Ruth's bed-and-breakfast in planning our pilgrimage to the Baseball Hall of Fame.

At this point, I had to pipe in. "Actually, I am conducting research on American inns and hope you don't mind if I ask a few quick questions like how long you have been here and how you went about getting established? By the way, everything so far has been perfectly delightful!" I took in the crown moldings and faded wallpaper around the dining room, uncertain that I could necessarily back up a statement about conducting research on American bed-and-breakfasts.

"Well, that's kind of an interesting story," replied Martin. "My wife and I are both retired college professors, and we took an early pension even though we were both tenured. It became clear that there was no room for advancement, especially with regard to our salaries. You know, I think you should speak with Ruth. She's finishing up the breakfast. She does all the cooking and baking."

Martin flipped back his chair. "Ruth, when you're finished preparing the eggs, can you please join us in the dining area to speak with these lovely guests!" He hollered back into the kitchen area, obviously an effort considering his soft-spoken nature.

Five minutes later, Ruth emerged from the kitchen wiping her hands on a flowery apron tied around her waist, complimenting her no-nonsense hairstyle and trousers. Ruth was about a foot shorter than her husband but sturdily built. One had the sense that she managed the nuts and bolts of the entire operation. "Hello, nice to meet you. Thank you for staying with us," she sighed as she took a seat. From close up, Ruth appeared to be worn out. Once she entered into the conversation, Martin retreated. "What would you like to know?" she asked.

I was experiencing déjà vu from my earlier conversation with the primary care physician at the Smith College award ceremony. Either I had a knack for finding stoic role models or no one, it seemed, ever gave the full story! And why should they? We as human beings construct elaborate, protective mechanisms to ward off being judged, being criticized, having our boundaries shaken, or as a friend of mine says, our cages rattled.

With regard to both the case of Ruth and the doctor, part of that defense was doling out the most generic advice possible—stuff you could look up. You can also see this variant of caution among newly referred patients, your obligation as the doctor to patiently tease out information layer by layer, sometimes with negligible results, till some degree of rapport is established.

"This is a very time-consuming business, but we enjoy our guests and try to make their stay as pleasant as possible," continued Ruth. "You may wish to review some of our literature in the living room. There you will find Chamber of Commerce information that may be useful, along with a listing of all the surrounding hospitality establishments. Take a look in the large red reference book on the coffee table. It's packed with useful information about inns in America." She sighed, "I don't mean to be rude, but I must go now and finish up." And with that Ruth stood up, adjusted her apron, and began clearing dishes.

My pipe dream of owning a cozy little bed-and-breakfast filled with hanging plants, interesting guests, and porcelain tea rests was deflated by a strong dose of reality. As with any other business, inn-keeping had a tedious side of daily upkeep, as inferred from Ruth's flattened verbal delivery and seeming exhaustion. It was the cursory online research that revealed steep start-up costs, an anticipated battle for a town variance, food and liquor licenses, and so forth.

Or maybe it was flipping through the mind-numbing red reference book sitting on the coffee table at that inn. There in those pages was every fact you could want to know about running an American inn but were afraid to ask: town permits, building variances, food and liquor licenses, application templates, appeals processes, furniture and equipment suppliers, staff recruitment agencies, employee benefit vendors, business and property insurance plans, a Q & A section, and pages upon pages of references—that instilled six degrees of intimidation.

Then it hit me front and center that any new career path would require overcoming robust start-up resistance in terms of researching the details, a process not unlike the starting of a medical practice. My father's philosophy emerged from somewhere deep within my subconscious as a gentle guidepost, rescuing me from the arduous details of the red reference book. He had always maintained that if you're not quite sure of what to change or do, stay the course.

My eyes welled up as I considered that in his own way, my father, along with my mother, had always tried to take care of his children during critical moments. Had my parents always advocated for the importance of being kind to yourself? Honestly, not always. That depended on the context. Sometimes grit and self-challenge were also called for. Dad believed, for instance, that everyone should strongly consider undergoing basic training of some sort to build character. Nevertheless, in deference to cognitively summoned parental wisdom, and on that very day, I opted to stay put as a doctor, at least for the time being.

I had to remind myself that enormous time and energy had been invested into first-rate medical training, so why sell myself short? I was proud of being a physician and pretty good at it! Evidently, the romanticized notion of running a bed-and-breakfast was not in the works right now. But joining a group practice, by contrast, was.

Table 2: A few details about running a private practice

	Nature of task	Responsible team member
Office policies	◦ Write a practice policy	◦ Doctor ◦ Office manager
Marketing	◦ Advertise your practice to everyone: colleagues, patients, families, the community. ◦ Establish an online presence.	◦ Web site ◦ Social media ◦ Hospital and Professional listings ◦ Person to person networking
Fees and collections	◦ Collect co-pays at each visit!	◦ Doctor ◦ Office manager ◦ Billing service
Risk management	◦ Provide clinical service within your comfort level. ◦ Seek supervision as needed.	◦ Doctor ◦ Risk manager.
The digital world	◦ Adapt electronic prescription capacity.	◦ Doctor ◦ Office manager ◦ Software vendor

Table 2: A few details about running a private practice continued

Telepsychiatry	◦ Use a secure telepsychiatry platform ◦ Be familiar with the mHealth App Landscape and learn about AI capacities.	◦ Doctor ◦ Office manager ◦ Software Vendor
Quality control	◦ Code and document visits accurately. Be prepared for insurance audits.	◦ Doctor ◦ Healthcare attorney
Stigma and resistance	◦ De-mystify psychiatry through building the doctor-patient rapport	◦ Doctor ◦ Office manager
Vacation coverage	◦ Line up trusted colleagues for vacation coverage. ◦ Offer a coverage stipend and be prepared to reciprocate.	◦ Vacation- a necessity, not a luxury!
IT support	◦ Work with a reputable and reliable IT specialist.	◦ Software vendor ◦ IT specialist

CHAPTER FIVE
Moving to Connecticut

I arrived in Connecticut to join a large multi-disciplinary practice six weeks prior to the Sandy Hook school massacre on December 14th, 2012. That unspeakable tragedy left twenty children and six adults dead, in addition to the shooter and his mother, who the shooter killed before traveling to the elementary school. Sandy Hook was not the last school massacre and was to be followed by a number of senseless mass shootings—an epidemic that continues to plague our country, a different conversation altogether. The fact that little children and heroic teachers were the victims of Sandy Hook was too much to bear.[10]

Within my new practice, the doctors and therapists teamed up with local authorities to provide on-site crisis intervention for the families of Sandy Hook's victims, as well as students, educational staff, and the surrounding Newtown community in need of mental health services. Our practice offered long-term counseling as well, but it was never entirely clear how many of those directly impacted by the shooting chose to continue receiving therapy services. Everyone was in complete shock and could not process the depth of their horror, the depth of their moral injury, nor believe that this quiet corner of the state had been so profoundly shaken. The atmosphere remained somber and subdued for many ensuing months.

Prior to my decision to exit New Jersey for Connecticut,

I had spent one whole afternoon lying on my back under the desk while on the phone with my IT specialist, Kevin. Together, Kevin and I installed a new router and all of its branch cables to secure a reliable internet connection.

This latest tech episode, despite Kevin's invaluable support and consistency, was probably the last straw—always needing to be a jack-of-all-trades. Solo practice was quickly losing its charm and this time, in contrast to the bed-and-breakfast pipedream, I was ready to make a meaningful change that would involve less administrative burden—thus the group setting. You could say that at this point, I was experiencing "transaction" fatigue. I was constantly adjusting to new regulations, new tech requirements, and steep insurance write-offs. By now, I had relocated my office from the Victorian house to an office building.

The posting of the Connecticut group practice position arrived at an opportune time. My husband and I discussed that we would spend weekends together in New Jersey while I worked in Connecticut during the week, and we would see how this arrangement worked out for the short term. We never anticipated that the new position would unfold amid an overwhelming national tragedy.

My decision to take the assignment also involved an element of nostalgia for New England. I liked the Connecticut locale, in obvious closer provenance to Massachusetts and Rhode Island than the middle Atlantic. Moving to New York for medical school had involved letting go of treasured Boston destinations like Union Oyster House as well as Newbury Street, now replaced by Lincoln Center and the borough of Manhattan embodying all of its power and excitement.

I really had no idea how long I would remain in Connecticut on this assignment. Too much time had elapsed putting down roots in New Jersey. Floating—not having the future completely mapped out and letting the experience unfold—was the solution!

I would find time to enjoy the offerings on the edge of New England adjacent to the Hudson Valley.

One evening, I headed toward the elevator in my hotel returning from the indoor swimming pool, modestly clad in a towel wrapped around my swimsuit, toga-style. That particular hotel would serve as my home away from home until I could find an apartment. I was living out of a suitcase and had never bothered to pack a robe.

The evening swim had become my therapy. En route to the elevator and situated on the left side of the hotel corridor, was a small conference center occupied with a trade show, vanilla and jasmine accents wafting into the hall. Hesitant in feeling underdressed, I kept walking, acknowledging that one could expect trade shows in a hotel. But at the elevator, I turned around to further check out the event.

"Join us," beckoned a pretty woman with a perky style, judged to be about my age and standing at the show's doorway entrance. "We hold these meetings every other Tuesday evening," she smiled, adding that her name was Bree, short for Brittanie. "Are you a hotel guest? How long do you plan to stay here?"

"You know, I'm not actually sure."

"Of course. No worries. I understand. As for me, I just live down the road so it's easy for me to show up every other Tuesday night for our beauty success meeting."

"Oh, beauty success meetings... well that's kind of different."

I now felt more at ease to expand on my circumstances noting that she seemed open, earnest, and had shared a little of her background.

"Actually, I am staying here at the hotel temporarily until I can find an affordable local rental. I just joined a group practice in the area. Sorry, you said Bree, right? As you can see, I am really not dressed for the occasion," I managed a smile, and suppressed a residual shiver from the swim. "Anyway, tell me more about your meeting."

Bree did not press me for work details and proceeded. "As I indicated, we are beauty consultants." She pointed to the conference room, which on closer look was laden with floral arrangements, ethereal cosmetic jars, fragrance bottles, and other display items that you might see in a department store. "And these are some of our wares. You can check everything out. Let me introduce you to Ella. Ella, how would you feel about treating this lady to our hand line." Bree was so self-assured, as she smoothly transferred me to the care of her colleague, Ella.

Before I knew it, Ella whisked me into the ladies room. This whole situation felt surreal—it was almost too easy to connect with these ladies, and everything was unfolding too rapidly!

"We always start every beauty experience with hand care. The eyes and hands are the windows into the soul." I overlooked the cliché.

"First you are going to apply this scrub for hand exfoliation. In doing so, you will remove the surface debris from the epidermal layer of your hands. This allows all the power ingredients that follow to more effectively permeate into the underlying dermal layer." Her voice was mesmerizing as she continued.

"And now, place your hands under the faucet to rinse with the warm water." My eyes grew heavy as I let down my guard. "Okay, please dry your hands. Last, you are going to apply this fragrance-free twelve-hour hand moisturizer followed by another emollient which locks in inter-cellular moisture and then you will tell me how your hands feel." Persuasive was she, Ella, with the polished, reassuring manner of a spa professional. She patiently awaited my feedback which took about five minutes to verbally formulate.

"Incredible. Just what I needed. My hands feel alive, but let's see, curiously heavy, and almost tingly. I am weirdly aware of the circulation. Really. I sincerely mean this, I am not just putting you on. Thank you. That was most considerate."

There was a release from fatigue, at this point physical as well as cognitive. True, I was less administratively burdened here than had been the situation in New Jersey. On the other hand, I was adjusting to a relinquishment of professional autonomy which felt unsettling. The group practice administrator was understandably now in charge, efficiently assigning patients who needed evaluation.

Being on the learning curve of my new caseload required intense daily concentration, perhaps leading to "empathy" or "listener burnout." Endemic to the field of psychiatry is listener fatigue, accompanied by low back pain, the latter a by-product of sitting in a poorly designed chair for eight hours at a clip. These are risks of the trade, and if you are a mental health provider, it is advisable to recognize and address these issues early on before they begin to mount and potentially affect your happiness.

Seeing upward of sixteen patients per day, I was navigating a ten-hour workday, a thirty-five-hour work week, plus the unpredictable weekly commute via Route 84, and the Garden State Parkway. I couldn't begin to relinquish my hotel, sad as it sounds, with its beloved swimming pool and sauna, the takeout dinners from nearby ethnic restaurants, the very decent available morning coffee, and the enduring commitment to a suitcase culture.

Allow me to digress that crossing the Tappan Zee Bridge was a counterintuitive driving experience, not for the geographically dyslexic. The original Tappan Zee was eventually replaced by The Governor Mario M. Cuomo Bridge, but in the year 2012, the Tappan Zee was still up and running during my Connecticut-New Jersey commute. In fact, you could track the weekly engineering progress of the Mario Cuomo cable by cable, if you were stuck on the Tappan Zee during rush hour.

To reach New Jersey from Connecticut, you had to proceed

north on Interstate 87, and, conversely, to reach Connecticut via New Jersey, you had to take I-87 South—in other words, it took a while to understand that I-87 South ultimately led you in a northerly direction and conversely, I-87 North led you south to the Garden State Parkway

On two separate occasions, I had accidentally recrossed the Hudson River on the Tappan Zee because of this interesting glitch. The first time, it was under the pressure of being punctual for the Connecticut practice interview. And the second time, well, let's just say that I was reminiscing with my daughter about the first driving mix-up while trying to transport her from our Berkshire vacation to her departing Newark Penn Station train.

And then, it happened again, in the middle of all this recounting. Instead of heading north for Newark Penn Station, there we were, recrossing the mighty Hudson south toward White Plains! Amid our silent panic, neither of us could help but appreciate the irony of the situation. After all, how many people do that: repeat the same driving mistake—in real time no less—while describing it? I suppose we can laugh over it now as part of the family lore. Miraculously, Victoria made her train that day.

Getting back to the hand demonstration with Ella, a sensation of tingling and heaviness radiated down the arms, and under the shoulders, a neuro-circulatory phenomenon sometimes described by patients during mindfulness relaxation, that is until her announcement, "The hand massage is concluded."

"May I ask you a question? Do you do this beauty business full time as your career? I mean how seriously do you take this?"

"Goodness," Ella replied. "Most of us have day jobs. I am a social worker on the staff of a special needs school. This is just a hobby business for me, my happy business, if you wish to call it that. Samantha, whom you are about to meet, however, is a full-time career beauty consultant. Honestly, I am not sure what all of the other beauty consultants do."

Ella and I returned to the trade-show room, Samantha now ready to take the helm.

"Let me guess, you are a beauty consultant," I commented to Samantha.

By now my name was known within the group. "Yes, Jane. In fact, I am the director of this unit."

Samantha was 30-something with passion and belief in her mission to make every woman on planet Earth look as beautiful as possible. She had grown up in Bangor, Maine—a city where, evidently, she did not foresee a future in a beauty career. Her bearing was patrician in that classic Louisa May Alcott manner.[11] Samantha, (everyone called her Sam) was tastefully dressed sporting a metallic gray jacket over a knee-length, fitted red dress, with multi-layered eye shadow, and black stiletto heels. Samantha was absolutely stunning, there was no question about it, embodying the essence of both New England and corporate elegance. She began to circulate among the display tables, describing the skincare lines and lifting various jars for emphasis.

"Listen Sam, I don't mean to be rude, but it's getting late, and I have to be up at the crack of dawn for work tomorrow, but thanks for your time anyway." I was dying to slip out of there.

Bree quickly intercepted. "Yep, it is late, and I totally respect that, so for you I have prepared a packet of skin care samples along with my business card. Please give the samples a try. That's all I request, your opinion. No obligation, I promise. May I call within a week, and we can go over everything? Yes? Deal?"

"Deal."

"Oh, I need to know how best to reach you!" I gave Bree my cell number. "Thanks. Smooches, honey! Have a great week!"

I registered the breeziness of our interchange, a studied contrast to the heftier workday conversations within the psychiatric practice. I acknowledged a craving for this type of easy camaraderie, feeling socially isolated in a new state, by choice, yes, and albeit in driving distance to New Jersey, but nevertheless alone.

There had to be more to life than whether certain assigned patients liked their doctor. I was learning that a side effect of practicing in a self-contained group practice, while, in many ways advantageous over solo practice, was the intense interpersonal climate which sometimes included receiving feedback from a team member not to your asking! My self-esteem was not going to be bound up in that type of pettiness. I knew my worth.

Bree had opened up a possibility for me, maybe even a sense of cautious optimism. Apparently, not everyone in these parts was reserved. Bree and the other ladies seemed lively enough, very confident in their savviness for business.

On the weekends when I stayed in Connecticut, extra time had emerged, a novelty for the working mom. Something felt pivotal—why not explore this whole beauty world, the perfect antidote for burnout and feeling isolated, filled with creative possibility.

Additionally, many of these ladies, like me, had responsible day jobs, presumably in business or healthcare which lent a certain level of gravitas to their side business in beauty. How difficult could beauty consulting be? After all, I had been sporting lip gloss, or as the French say, *brillant a levres,* since high school.

CHAPTER SIX
Opting Into the Beauty World

Three months after diligently applying Bree's samples, I noticed a subtle improvement in my complexion. There was an evenness of skin tone, expression lines were softened, and in general, there was more radiance. Could this be possible in such a short time?

With much trepidation, I took the dive and opened my own little beauty business. There was certainly enough support being surrounded with seasoned and personable beauty consultants like Sam, Bree, and Ella, all available as entrepreneurial role models. Maybe we would become friends, and this little business could provide a counterbalance to potential negativity. At the time, I viewed beauty consulting as transient, another adventure, another notch on the belt of experience, and an activity to pass the time in the evenings and over the weekends, certainly nothing too serious.

My random entrée into the beauty world is typical of so many beauty consultants, at least the ones I have interviewed. A successful beauty consultant, sales director and one of my supportive mentors, who preferred anonymity, related that her background was in finance, and she had no intention of becoming a beauty consultant. However, like me, she began to experiment with the company's product lines, liked the results, and over time, took over a colleague's beauty business, adding "I was impressed by the process of self-promotion. Unlike other business venues, here I could rise to the top if I really wanted to without any insurmountable barriers."

For me, as a respected doctor, the trickiest part of this new adventure would be marketing my new business to friends and family without sending them all into septic shock. Most women psychiatrists that I knew coped with burnout through more conventional means like moving into leadership positions within professional organizations, the American Psychiatric Association being one, or securing teaching appointments on medical faculties. In other words, they created professional variety.

I had already served in organizational leadership as a chapter president and honestly did not have aspirations of climbing further to assume a national post. For leisure, my colleagues might choose to travel, to embrace yoga or another sport, to add in a weekly card game or monthly book club.

Yet beauty consulting? Doubtful. Not a chance that any of those women psychiatrists, my peers, had ventured down this avenue.

The conversation with my mother would hypothetically unfold with me posing a question. "Mom, are you sitting down?" I would pause, inhale, and exhale. "Listen, I have started selling skin care sets."

My mother would respond, "What? You're kidding. I can't picture this. You've worked so hard to become a physician. I mean it sounds kind of interesting and certainly different. But it also sounds a little crazy, Jane. Well, come to think of it, you've been at psychiatry for a while. I guess I can understand why you might want to try something different at this point. Have you thought of going back and doing another residency in family practice, like Dad suggested?"

I could hear my mother's train of thought ticking away as I suppressed an internal scream. Mom had obviously been unable to empathize with my "plight," and frankly, had a limited idea of the work, energy, and sacrifice that goes into completing a single residency program, despite her well-meaning intentions and compassionate nature.

Typical of women in her generation who had lived through the Great Depression, my mother's idea of a beauty regimen consisted of the weekly coiffure and manicure at the salon, which, of course, included chit-chat with her hair stylist-plus red lipstick daily applied from an ornate gilded compact. In the morning, by Mom's standard, you washed your face for the day with bar soap, concluding the skin care portion.

Moreover, everyone, including my mother, viewed me as a devoted doctor, and for all I knew held a strong idea that the medical world and the beauty world were not compatible. From that perspective, managing the two worlds was understandably a stretch. There would be resistance from directions not yet anticipated, and how best to brand myself as both a respected, nonfrivolous doctor within the medical community and a capable beauty consultant in the world at large would continue to present itself as my number one challenge.

Prospective customers would be scheduled during evenings and weekends, the goal to promote the skin care line, with perhaps a makeup application thrown in. In the beauty industry, makeup is never called "makeup" but rather "a glamour application." I confess that my nerves were high for that first appointment, booked with a psychiatric social worker from the practice. She arrived early at my newly rented flat.

I had managed to humanize my place by hanging drapes, purchasing a sofa and coffee table, and setting up attractive houseplants. A round glass consulting table, covered with a beige tablecloth, served as the room's focal point, this day beautifully adorned with product jars, a bouquet of flowers spilling over into the center, and the table positioned just right to capture the late afternoon sun. A comfortable chair and mirror were provided for my guest. I had studied the various table setups of Bree and Sam during our beauty get-togethers and had opted for the ethereal look.

In fact, Bree and Sam had provided invaluable hands-on beauty training, particularly during the biweekly success meetings where we would review new products and their age-fighting ingredients, along with business strategies and how to find new customers using tools and resources provided by the company.

The meetings had relocated from my hotel to a nearby multi-purpose lounge within an upscale condo development. Sam generated optimistic themes like best table display, fragrance sampling, and a guaranteed closing with your prospective new customer. There was a definite structure and creativity to these meetings. The beauty consultants and their guests would initially sample every product on display artistically laid out along the marble countertop.

Sam would then assemble the group for a lecture on her favorite product of the month, such as a new lifting serum—its ingredients, its benefits, plus her own sales wisdom thrown in. She would quiz us on her talk to make certain we had been listening. I had never met anyone so captivated with skincare products! She embraced them all with open arms—the serums, exfoliating agents, the "eaux de toilette"—much like an extended family, her enthusiasm was contagious. And then the party would begin with networking, edibles, and a chance to catch up with the other beauty consultants.

At nine o'clock sharp, Sam would bid us adieu, pitching a weekly sales challenge for the next meeting which included an incentive or prize. The challenge might entail adding two new customers to your bookings or bringing a guest to the next meeting.

I was already thinking about where to locate prospective customers: vendors, perhaps one or two people from the psychiatric practice, and even the hospitality staff I had befriended at my hotel. Whatever Sam's challenge happened to be, I left those meetings feeling energized, empowered, and happy.

And so, I welcomed my new customer into the apartment with a warm and friendly glow.

"Welcome Sylvie! Thanks for keeping our appointment today. I know you are very busy, and your being here will help me learn and grow as a beauty consultant. I would like to introduce you to a four-part skincare program with eleven reputed benefits. Can you imagine? Eleven antiaging benefits! Each of the four components works synergistically to promote a youthful complexion, line reduction, added moisture, added firmness, and protection against environmental toxins such as the UVA/UVB radiation from the sun and poor air quality. You, of course, are free to sample any of the other items on display, but I recommend that we initially focus on the skincare set, just four easy steps from left to right samples while I explain. The first step is to cleanse and exfoliate the face, the second to apply a moisturizer, the third to apply a customized sunscreen on either the right or left side of your face as you prefer, and the last step is to apply a replenishing antiaging serum on the other side of the face."

"That sounds delightful. Let's go for it!" said Sylvie.

"May I ask, what are your goals for your skin and our consultation today? What areas of your face do you feel need attention? For many people, it's the undereye area, as the skin there is more delicate and tends to more readily manifest signs of age and stress."

"I'm not really sure yet, but it all sounds terrific!" Sylvie replied.

Sylvie sat down, completed a survey card, and then with gusto proceeded to sample the entire smorgasbord of toners, fragrance, and moisturizers in her own random order, rather than following my suggestion to sequentially sample the skin care set.

My impression soon became that the less I spoke the better would be our rapport, as Sylvie seemed like the type of shopper who barrels through merchandise, making quick yes/no decisions.

And so, I took note of her preferences and occasionally offered complimentary feedback. Sylvie even tried a few lip shades, which for her seemed like a guilty indulgence, as she had shared that she did not really wear makeup. After one hour's time, Sylvie abruptly arose, thanked me for my time, and vanished without so much as making a purchase.

I was dumbfounded! Had I inadvertently offended Sylvie? As naive as this may sound, that visit was supposed to launch my beauty career. I had fantasies of Sylvie, and other new customers, buying out my entire inventory and making enough referrals to boost my fledgling business.

Alas, so much for the adage that people shop with their fingers, or any of the other senses for that matter. In later reviewing that embarrassing debut with Bree and Sam, I discovered that disappointing outcomes happen and are all part of the game. Meeting the seemingly enthusiastic customer who does not make a purchase is buried within the war chest of every beauty consultant. The beauty consultant must then go back and, in sales terminology, work even harder with the next customer "to overcome objections."

Back at the psychiatry practice, my relationship with Sylvie, having crisscrossed from work colleague to prospective beauty customer then back again to work colleague, became quietly strained. But as two committed professionals, we managed to work through it, or around it, always keeping our relationship polite but at bay. We never mentioned the beauty consultation again, my guess that she was not comfortable with having allowed herself one hour of pure indulgence. Moving forward, I vowed that "church and state," "beauty and medicine," would forever remain in separate quarters.

Susan, a seasoned, accomplished beauty consultant who happens to be my sales director, shared some thoughts during a conversation. "Being successful as a consultant in the beauty world parallels success in many other retail endeavors. You need the need, and the ability to talk with strangers."

Resilience might be added to Susan's success list, that is the ability to handle rejection, turn around, and approach the next prospective customer with a clean slate. Whether this is a learned coping skill or built into the internal wiring of the consultant is up for discussion, but I can tell you that the most successful beauty consultants all have it.

Susan believes that the reasons why people become beauty consultants are:
- ♡ Recognition
- ♡ Friendship
- ♡ Money
- ♡ Ability to set up your own workflow and space

Susan adds, "Sales empowers women. If you are willing to learn, you will become a different person. Public speaking, for instance, is a part of it. Plus, you develop confidence, talent, a better appearance, networking, and creating conversation. Look at how confident you've become, Jane. I can see it!"

Interesting! Friendship and lifestyle balance were definitely my go-to reasons, but not necessarily for Susan. She had emigrated to the East Coast from California, only to discover upon arriving that her husband wanted a divorce. Now single with young children to feed and clothe, Susan connected with a supportive sales director, became a sales director herself, and proceeded to build a lucrative cosmetic business. For Susan, financial security and workplace autonomy appeared to be the top priorities.

Over time, my selling competence increased, as did, ironically, my skill as a doctor. I became adept at compartmentalizing beauty consulting, making certain to avoid discussing cosmetics with any patients, and, conversely, playing down my medical background with the beauty customers. After all, who wants to hear Dr. Otto Kernberg's views of the borderline personality structure during a facial?[12]

During psychiatry hours, my interviewing technique with patients underwent a subtle shift, now more nuanced and less formulaic, less classic textbook, but by no means perfect. Logically, you could reason that it may have just been a matter of cumulative experience, as, over time, all healthcare professionals improve their interviewing technique. But outside the protective walls of the medical office, I was in the public arena along with everyone else, and, like them, navigating the uncertainties of the real world. Beauty consulting was certainly humbling!

Beauty consultants are instructors, not makeup artists nor cosmetologists. People do not always get this. In New Jersey, for example, a student must log twelve hundred educational hours, translating to a course of approximately fifteen weeks, in order to be eligible for a cosmetology license. Other states are comparable in their requirements ranging from one thousand to two thousand one hundred hours of instruction. For beauty consultants without a cosmetic license this translates to not applying any products on a customer's face.

I was as diligent as humanly possible in adhering to the no-touch rule, guiding the customer to perform their own facial, using diagrams, videos, company mobile apps, and, where necessary, my own face to demonstrate the product lines. Bree, in addition to being a beauty consultant, is a certified makeup artist. She had commented, To see the change in a vulnerable person premakeup, after the glamour application, they look finished. They feel attractive, happy with their reflection. That, for me, is better than anything."

My taste in glamour has always been subtle, and therefore I promoted nuance for all my beauty customers which actually pleased them. The key to everyday makeup is to look like you are not wearing any makeup. This might be a counterintuitive statement, but it reflects my beauty philosophy and therefore requires high caliber products.

I quickly became adept at locating where on the customer's face to focus, generally around the eye or in the lip area. Accenting both areas simultaneously could create a glamour traffic jam, rendering a clownish appearance. And if the skin was not adequately hydrated, forget about products going on smoothly or looking luxurious. In fact, within the beauty world, the skin is considered a blank canvas in terms of applying glamour. Akin to painting, the canvas must be properly primed for the artist to begin the painting.

I guided my customers to what I believed were the polychromatic eye shadows and lip shades, as variegated hues tend to create a more authentic application. If you think about it, most coloring in the natural world is not monochromatic, and therefore makeup that replicates nature is a notch above in quality.

Lipstick, for example, whether marketed as rose, pink, or burgundy, that contains undertones of brown, gives a sophisticated finish. My favorite combination encompassed various hues of ivory, beige, and brown skillfully blended over the eyelid with hints of berry or autumn in the lip area. I developed multiple versions of this look—optimal, in theory, for those with hazel eyes, but looking quite fantastic on just about every woman who became my customer.

Table 3:
Top twelve reasons why a cosmetic sale does not close

Customer's lack of interest in beauty product(s)	Meeting held out of politeness, but priorities lie elsewhere
Use of a competing brand	Willingness to compare products
History of product allergies	Avoidance of any new products
Financial considerations	On a fixed budget
Aversion to product(s)	Shade, texture, fragrance, difficulty of application, packaging characteristics
Concern with ingredients	Holistic and/or fragrance-free preference
Serviced by another specialist	Established during consultation
Cultural factors	Attention to beauty care in conflict with norms and beliefs
Cognitive factors	Negative self-perception and low self-esteem
Beauty consultant factors	Failure to build rapport or demonstrate sufficient product knowledge
Customer readiness	More time needed with exposure to product(s)
Lack of time	Beauty regimen too time-consuming for customer's lifestyle

CHAPTER SEVEN
Beauty is Holistic

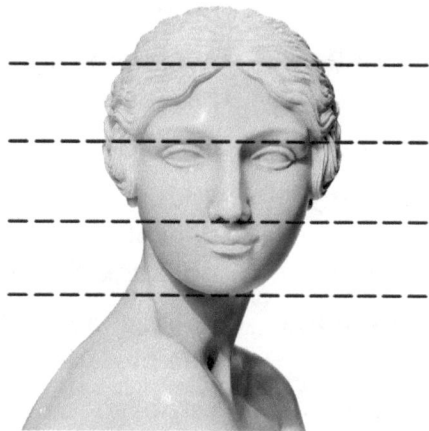

The Ancient Greeks divided the human face into horizontal thirds. Each third—the superior, from the hairline to the eyes, the middle, from the eyes to the upper lip, and the lower part, from the upper lip to the tip of the chin, had to be of equal mathematical dimension to create the perfect symmetry. The width of the face was ideally two-thirds of the length. For the face to represent the ideal in beauty, it also had to be accompanied by a beautiful persona beyond physical characteristics. One must credit the ancient Greeks for being holistic and progressive in their thinking, viewing beauty as a harmony between the mind and body.[13]

Since the ancient Greeks, the subject of beauty has been a hot-button topic, fraught with ambivalence, debated and tossed around in various cultural crosscurrents.

How many women plausibly spend more time and money on their gardens than on their face, maybe not organized around the fact that the skin is the largest organ in the human body? They may hold the belief that the skin will take care of itself, and nature will take its course—so why fret? Such cosmetic fatalism is not the whole picture, however. The complexion, like the cardiopulmonary system, the musculature and metabolism, requires maintenance, investment of time, a basic wellness program to remain vital, regardless of a person's age or sociodemographic status. From my platform as a beauty consultant, I advocate tending to the complexion. That said, I do not wish to offend my friends and family who have amazing gardens! Gardens are also important and not mutually exclusive with cosmetics.

For Autumn Whitefield-Madrano, author of *Face Value: The Hidden Ways Beauty Shapes Women's Lives,* the subject of beauty is fraught with contradiction. The daughter of a feminist-oriented mother, raised at NOW meetings and later an intern at *Ms. Magazine,* Whitefield-Madrano describes an embattled relationship with cosmetics, "makeup," in her words. On one hand, she admits to loving the process of makeup application. On the other hand, she is open about feeling like she is betraying the feminist cause with a mascara wand.

She believes that "Beauty invites gaps in our thinking . . . between how people look and how we aspire to look. . . between appearance standards of men and those for women . . . . For decades these inconsistencies have been acknowledged for their negative effect on our lives . . . in the face of idealized, retouched, impossibly perfect images—or that beauty rituals are a trap, distracting women from what really matters."[14]

Face Value reflects the point-counterpoint debate of the 1990s wherein Naomi Wolf expounded *The Beauty Myth* and Nancy Etcoff countered with *Survival of the Prettiest,* two diametrically opposed viewpoints of the beauty world.

Feminism was on track with women working around the clock for equality in all walks of life: education, the workplace, household balance, reproductive rights, and adequate childcare. Wolf argued that the beauty industry was predicated on maintaining an archaic social order, keeping women oppressed, slaves to their appearance in the quest for sexual acceptance. Etcoff, by contrast, argued that the strive for beauty is quintessentially part of human nature, basic to species survival and should not be conflated with political manipulation.[15]

Another contributor to this topic, Medard Hilhorst, classifies human beauty along seven domains: a) physical attributes, b) external attire and accoutrements, c) the overall impression, d) postural carriage and performance, e) personal appeal, f) interpersonal skill set, and g) likability. Using Hilhorst's classification system as a didactic exercise and allowing for category overlap, an individual who presents an artistic aura and happens to be interesting and stylish would embody items c, g, and b—artistic in impression, engaging in manner, and stylish in attire.

They are therefore considered to have a beauty that transcends their physical attributes, a point so overrepresented that it has been incorporated into our basic, household ethos—always look beyond the surface, for beauty is holistic.[16]

Regarding Wolf's perspective of beauty as cultural enslavement, let's get real. The motivation to look good is for one's own sake and not an indicator of cultural oppression. Her hypothesis is dated. Just look around. Women choose to look good for themselves. Notice all the amazing, accomplished women out there who pay homage to their appearance, as do men and individuals identified as nonbinary.

Cultivation of a healthy lifestyle and the embracing of a modern beauty style abound. This does not imply undue vanity or compromise in personal or professional integrity. We have integrated beauty care into wellness, believing that the skin deserves the same attention as physical metabolism and fitness.

With the passage of time, we have moved beyond viewing self-care as a guilty indulgence, a value that was unfairly etched into the female psyche for decades. The current standard for what is considered beautiful is flexible and varied and embraces a broad range of styles while embedded in the higher objective of health and wellbeing.[17] The reasonable person attends to their appearance for their own sake, not necessarily for the sake of vanity or a social agenda. In that regard, we have circled back to the holistic philosophy of ancient Greece.

Does the beauty industry understand this? The anonymously mentioned beauty sales director certainly believes so. For her, there is no intrapsychic conflict. When asked if the beauty world is empowering or intimidating, she responds "People elevate themselves. One way is through beauty. You get your hair done; your face done. It's self-care. Self-care is very important . . . . Cosmetics address the exterior. You also have to care for yourself internally. I believe in a homeopathic approach. As a beauty consultant, I touch people's lives. I create transformation when I [introduce] someone to a product."

In her training classes, this director instructs that first and foremost, the consultant must obtain a skin history from their client. She strongly advocates using a structured questionnaire, often provided by the company. The questionnaire builds professionalism and reinforces an interpersonal boundary between consultant and customer. It accurately records the customer's concerns and preferences and then guides the consultant in making future recommendations moving forward.

For example, how would the person characterize their skin—dry, normal, sensitive, or oily? What are their goals for skin care? How much time and money are they willing to put into looking good? How concerned are they about signs of aging?

Where do they identify the problematic areas of their face? How would they like their overall complexion to look—hydrated, radiant, even-toned, firm, smooth, or blemish-free? In other words, what are their skincare priorities?

How does the customer feel about adding in glamour, such as extenders and finishers? For clarification, extenders, also called primers, maintain the wearable longevity of a glamour product such as eye shadow or foundation, analogous to a medication's duration of action within the human body. Finishers, on the other hand, such as setting powders and finishing sprays, lock in the look. Returning to the customer, what products are they currently using and what has been an effective regimen?

What is their allergy history? If positive, what was the allergen and what happened? Product allergies are common, particularly as people age. Is there a history of nut or food allergies? Skincare products can draw on olive, nut, and sesame-based ingredients, plus a host of items from the plant world.

The language of this ever-changing beauty industry has become an anchor, as would be expected for someone learning any new discipline. Words like power ingredients, radiance, hydration, and expression lines refer to skincare objectives, while terms like cupid's bow, the tail of the eyebrow, along with the foundation properties of matte, luminous, and natural fall within the domain of glamour. Some of the key power ingredients are hyaluronic acid, glycolic acid, Vitamins B3, C, and E, and retinol. While each has unique benefits, the ultimate objective is to combat aging through the boosting of collagen and protecting the surface skin from environmental hazards that contribute to aging.

The desired result? A flawless face, or close to flawless, of course. Colors are shades of hues with poetic sounding names, like peacock shimmer or dusky horizon. Humectants, emollients, and occlusives are each a different type of moisturizer and each with a unique function. Humectants bulk up the skin's surface moisture, emollients smooth out the skin, and occlusives, as the name suggests, block the escape of moisture by creating a protective film over the skin. After a while, these terms glide off the tongue as if you are now multilingual. It is essential to have a working comfort with this vocabulary in order to be taken seriously by your customer and fellow beauty consultants.

Table 4: Skin moisturizers, a primer

Type	Action	Examples
Humectants	Restores moisture to the surface of the skin	♡ Glycerin ♡ Ceramides
Emollients	Smooths the skin, including rough and dry areas	♡ Plant and fruit oils ♡ Food sources: grapes, avocados, almonds, sunflowers
Occlusives	Prevents the escape of moisture by creating a film over the skin	♡ Mineral Oil ♡ Paraffin

When a new beauty customer sits down, I draw on skills learned from my psychiatric training. Maybe this is pushing the envelope, but the beauty consultant is like a physician, listening carefully and compassionately. After all, the customer is disclosing very intimate aspects of their appearance, in this instance a self-evaluation of their face and complexion, a potentially delicate subject, beset with self-critical thinking and cognitive distortions carried over from childhood. The goal is to build rapport and create a judgment-free beauty zone all while gathering information.

For a psychiatrist like me, one of the most intriguing aspects of beauty training is cultivating an effective communication style during the cosmetic consultation, acknowledging the customer's skin care goals and general persona. The parallels to psychiatry lie in the speed and flexibility required during the client interaction. The beauty consultant might notice if the customer is in a rush, if they have an open or fixed budget, if they love or eschew product information, if they feel guilty for spending time on themselves, or if they want to confide in you—all part of your professional judgment.

A guarantee of result, as in psychiatry, is never offered. A small percentage of beauty customers may request detailed product information above and beyond the company's package insert, akin to the patient's need to comb the internet before trying a new medication. Customers, as they should be, are savvy and have become increasingly aware of potentially controversial ingredients such as methylparaben, an antibacterial product preservative loosely linked to hormonal imbalance and cancer.

Early in my beauty training, I conducted a group demonstration for ten to twelve women at their assisted living facility. Each guest sampled a prearranged tray of cleansers, moisturizers, and concealers, with several making purchases. A few days later, I called the guests to follow up on their experience, and the most enthusiastic customer during the event lamented to me that after applying her new moisturizer, she broke out in a rash.

Naturally, I felt terrible. I promised her a refund. Had she consulted with her primary physician? If she wished, I would speak with the primary care doctor. I advised her to discard the offending product after receiving a refund and also called the company for their advice, but I couldn't do much beyond that. The rash was most likely an allergic reaction. The point is that my doctor instincts kicked in, approaching the problem as a concerned physician.

Skin care samples are distributed to the customer, much like in medical practice, where a week's worth of pharmaceutical samples can be dispensed while introducing a new medication. When the beauty customer tries the sample, they are often able to make an immediate decision about whether to purchase the product based on how it looks and how it feels on their skin. One of the most common concerns that I have encountered is unhappiness with the undereye appearance: circles, darkening, and puffiness. The customer then applies the eye product as directed, followed by a concealer. They glance in the mirror and feel a sense of hopeful renewal—that this new regimen will boost their confidence.

Purchasing decisions may be based on the physical characteristics of the product: the packaging, fragrance, and feel. If the customer believes their beauty consultant is sincere, and not just trying to make a buck, they will generally become loyal customers, maybe not making an initial purchase but over time investing in a sensible skin care regimen. I cannot tell you how many times my sales director told me to wait it out with any given customer when I would call Susan in frustration, and voilà she was always correct.

One of my favorite types of consultation is with the busy corporate executive. Not to stereotype, but sometimes high-powered women in leadership positions allow you, the beauty consultant, to make all the decisions.

I recall a consultation with a corporate attorney, Marsha, in her office. For that meeting, I had decided to power dress, looking particularly sharp in a high-fashion blouse, skirt, and jacket trio. I added heels, plus artisanal jewelry in keeping with my eclectic style, and, of course, makeup, perfectly applied. I had rehearsed my presentation with scientific precision the previous night and had conducted sufficient product research to confidently field most scientific inquiries that might arise.

Here's how things went:

"Hi Jane, come on in. Just have to make one quick phone call. Why don't you set up over there while I finish this conversation. It's okay, you can stay in the office during the call." Marsha indicated a small, precarious-looking sofa. I was uncertain as to whether it would support my display. Okay, so the tray and beauty jars would wobble a bit. If Marsha was happy, so was I.

Marsha hung up the phone and emerged from behind her desk to perch on a chair adjacent to the display, intensely studying the setup of a mirror inserted into a small tray, and skin set samples plus eye cream samples, all sequentially arranged in the tray wells over a decorative towel that I had spread to protect her sofa.

Whipping out my trusty diagram saved from medical school, I began. "The skin has three layers, the outermost epidermis, the middle dermal layer, and the underlying hypodermal layer. Within the epidermis, there are five stratum spanning from nearest to the surface to the underlying dermal layer: the stratum corneum, the stratum lucidum, the stratum granulosum, the stratum spinosum, and the stratum basale. But it's the dermal layer wherein lies all the action in terms of the products' antiaging and therapeutic properties, as we are going to demonstrate."

I took a quick inhale. "You can think of the dermal layer as vital scaffolding that holds up the face, with the aid of elastin and collagen, analogous to the construction of a building. The hypodermal layer, of course, also has important physiologic functions—"

By now, Marsha, who had finished sampling the tray components, cut me off.

"Okay, Jane, that's enough. I get it. Listen, I want two of those complete skin care sets, two of those eye creams—I like those! A cranberry and a coral lipstick, black mascara, two eye shadows—you select the shades for me—I trust you and whatever else you think I need to look absolutely gorgeous. I have an important professional dinner tomorrow night and I need to look good, I mean really good! Not to be disrespectful, but I literally have two more minutes till my next conference call, so if you need payment information, here's my card. You can process everything right outside in the waiting room."

Then Marsha chuckled. "And please, come back into my office, allow me to take a glance and sign the invoice so you can get paid, and I can get my card back." Marsha, enthralled with the eye cream, had already reapplied it under the eyes three times. In fact, it was beginning to look gloppy.

Such trust, in essentially flinging her credit card at me. I was both honored and floored! Here we were easily talking about over a $350 dollar retail order which I considered a straightforward, almost too easy consultation. From Marsha's standpoint this beauty investment was a financial drop in the bucket, plus I had ostensibly saved her valuable time from brick-and-mortar retail shopping, thus freeing up her energy for her career and whatever else was her priority.

All in all, I had earned that commission through responsive service. I would make sure to include a generous gift with purchase. In the coming years, I would take diligent care of Marsha, tactfully inquiring about her life, her cosmetic preferences, her wish for follow ups and makeovers for special occasions, all while making certain to ask for referrals, as referrals are the backbone of your cosmetic business.

It is advisable to respect the limits of your beauty expertise when working with customers. If their question feels overwhelming, it probably is. Beauty consultants are instructed to refer customers to dermatologists or their primary care doctors for medically related skincare conditions such as rosacea or acne.

This may seem obvious, especially for a psychiatrist like me trained to work collaboratively with other medical specialists, but you can quickly get over your pay grade, especially since customers often tell their beauty consultant far more about themselves than they would share with their physician or even their psychiatrist.

Being responsible, mindful, and adhering to company guidelines are the appropriate safeguards within the beauty industry. Never criticize a competing company. The top companies all produce effective product lines. Customers often do comparison shopping and compositely assemble the beauty regimen that works for them, selecting from multiple companies. And if you will allow me to state the obvious, do not forget that this is a happy business, so keep it light. I try not to discuss my personal problems with beauty customers, nor with my psychiatric patients for that matter!

Table 5: An annotated beauty timeline

Ancient Greece (c. 428–348 BCE): Beauty is rooted in mathematical aesthetics, according to the Fibonacci ratio or the divine proportion, corresponding to the number 1.618. The Fibonacci ratio states that if a line is divided unequally, the ratio of longer to the shorter segment should equal that of the entire line to the longer segment. This principle is employed by the sculptor, Phidias, and permeates throughout the ancient Greek beauty ideal.

Ancient Rome (c. 753 BCE–476 CE): Principles of symmetry and proportion are carried over from Ancient Greece. In addition, while skin care is emphasized, makeup is understated to preserve female virtue. Fragrance becomes important, as does the use of mineral ingredients. Kohl (derived from ashes) is used for dark eye liner, malachite (a green-hued mineral derived from copper) for green eye shadow, and azurite (a deep-blue mineral also derived from copper) for blue eye shadow.

 **The Empiricist Movement (c. 1690s–1800):** Philosophers Addison, Reid, Burke, Alison, Hume, and to a certain degree, Kant, fundamentally join in to shift the beauty template from objective to subjective. Beauty is in the eye of the beholder. For David Hume "beauty (is) an expression of a subjective order that reflects our nature, customs, or capricious inclinations."

 **The Victorian/Edwardian Era (c. 1890s–1920s):** "The Gibson Girl" persona emerges from the sketches of the artist Charles Dana Gibson and comprises features such as the hourglass physique, athleticism, poise, independence, and a youthful visage. The hair is piled into a high coiffure. Despite an attempt to unburden women and broaden their roles in the world, the Gibson girl image, at least from the twenty-first century vantage, suggests an elitism and exclusivity, setting an unrealistic bar for Edwardian beauty.

 **The 1950s and 60s:** Hollywood glamour reigns supreme with the Marilyn Monroe prototype at the helm. Hair is platinum, makeup is flamboyant, and curves are in.

 **The 1970s:** The Feminist movement takes hold, hair reverting to its natural hue, flower childlike garments gracefully flowing, and pants now the everyday norm. Authenticity and self-expression are encouraged, everyone asserting their unique style.

The millennium: The ethnic beauty market flourishes between 2001–2010, the beauty industry addressing diversity and the cosmetic needs of African American, Hispanic, and Asian American populations. Models are inclusive, drawn from a variety of ethnic backgrounds accurately reflecting the consumer composition of the United States.

Contemporary trends: Virtually anything goes. Hair color encompasses a wide range, tattoos are a form of self-expression, and fashion styles remain free-floating. Women are encouraged to embrace their own bodies and stay active. Skin care is self-care. Glamour products are subtle, color enhancements artfully applied and individually blended.

CHAPTER EIGHT
In Praise of Beauty

Welcome, welcome, welcome! As your director, I'm your business adviser. However, you will set your own goals—this is your business. You're on your own but never alone . . . be patient with yourself. You will not learn everything overnight . . . success is often a "fail forward" experience. It's getting a handle on who you are and what you want, then discipline yourself to work toward that goal using good time management. The key? Well, that's in you!

This is an excerpt from the first letter I ever received from my sales director, Susan. She went on to outline the various initiatives needed for beauty success such as offering a gift with every purchase or gift with every consultation, and apologized for the delay in sending her letter, hoping to meet me soon, implying that beauty consulting is not for everyone. Alone in my apartment, I was touched while rereading the letter. Someone with the business acumen of Susan demonstrated a caring as reflected in the letter that showed genuine warmth and personal interest, in my estimation unusual for corporate America. Susan has continued to be an outstanding director, always present, generous, objective, and, of course, strategic in promotional ideas that may boost customer interest and sales revenue.

Allow me to return to an earlier point, this time with ten years of beauty consulting and fifteen Star Consultant awards under my belt. What does it take to be successful in beauty sales? As with any other type of sales, the bottom line is verve. The company calls it "warm chatter," quickly establishing a link with the new acquaintance who may or may not become your customer.

Being persuasive and confident also come in handy. Many beauty consultants open with a perky line such as, "You know, you are the sharpest gal in the room today. I couldn't help but notice how together you look. Would you be offended if I give you my business card and get your opinion on a few products . . . no obligation of course."

Who doesn't love a compliment? Compliments make the person's whole day, especially when delivered with conviction. But as a physician I simply cannot do this, especially with new acquaintances! Psychiatric training theoretically involves just the opposite. Stay neutral wherever possible, form an alliance with your patient's capacity for self-observation, and lead your patient to their own hopeful conclusions. Interpret your patient's need for constant reassurance and praise as an ego defense.

At the risk of overstatement, this issue is a reminder that I am forever stuck between these two rock and hard place cultures—getting excited in the beauty world versus staying measured and neutral in the psychiatric world. For instance, at the conclusion of a sales convention the surcharge emanating from those heartfelt beauty directors quickly dissipates in the car ride home from Atlantic City, or on the airplane back from Minneapolis, or from wherever it was that we all convened.

My private conversation with myself might proceed in this fashion: "Hmm . . . I really don't see myself pulling off the initiative in that sales director's speech. Calling everyone in my phone contacts? That would give me a serious panic attack. What if these people hang up on me? I couldn't bear the humiliation of listening to a dead phone line. After all, I am a respected doctor. People do not hang up on me, that's not okay. Fine for her, or the second sales director up there on the podium but, God no, not for me." I am now feeling quite certain that I have talked myself out of most of the initiatives outlined at the sales convention.

How did this happen? Those speeches were so compelling, obviously intended to pump up the sales force. One inspiring story after the next was delivered from the podium, the American dream personified, women arriving in this country with nothing on their backs except ambition. These were strong, determined women who evidently built a fulfilling life as sales directors through the selling of cosmetics. Or perhaps they were tired of corporate culture and needed to alter their career track.

From audience to stage and all around the convention hall was a cross section of the United States, women from all ethnicities, geographic locations, and walks of life. Sometimes, there were a few male beauty consultants sprinkled in, who, in my opinion, deserved a standing ovation, a special badge of recognition for their courage in breaking down the social barriers. I literally wanted to get up from my seat and give those gentlemen a huge hug. Hats off to nonbinary beauty consultants as well. It's hard enough doing this beauty gig as a woman, but it takes exceptional talent and dedication to conduct a cosmetic sales business from an alternative and unique perspective.

While I appreciate the ease with which some beauty consultants line up bookings, on occasion with total strangers in hotel lobbies, supermarkets, and on commuter trains, I have developed my own cautious technique which generally involves getting a product opinion from a personal acquaintance. Maybe this is too cautious a strategy that will never catapult me to the convention stage, footlights aglow, but all things considered this is within my comfort level. The customer is not rejecting me, they are rejecting the opportunity to try a new product.

Although, come to think of it, on one occasion, I did a spur-of-the-moment beauty consultation in a hotel lobby with three strangers. My scheduled prospective customer, a ballet instructor by day and tarot card reader by night, stood me up. There I was, sitting in the lobby with my beauty briefcase, all dressed up one blustery Saturday afternoon in March without a booking. All of a sudden, a group of three women, evidently noting my cosmetic briefcase and styled appearance, approached me. They were from out of town, and in three hours were apparently due to attend a wedding soiree.

"So, we saw your suitcase, or official tote bag, or whatever you call it," exclaimed the most extroverted lady, "and we thought, 'Oh, what the hell! She looks like a nice lady who might be able to give us a few makeup tips,' though in my case it's probably hopeless. We have the gowns and shoes hanging up in our hotel room, but nothing to put on our precious little faces.

"Are you from around here? I bet you are. You look like a sort of Jersey-girl lite and it looks like you just kind of got stood up. We saw you taking out your phone several times. Maybe you were trying to contact your customer. Whatever happened seems pretty rotten!"

Inwardly, I cringed while maintaining an outwardly forced smile. Was my disappointment that obvious? Then, continuing to keep my cool and laughing off her observation, I explained that I was not a makeup artist, but would be happy to help the three ladies prepare for their event.

Two hours later, each lady had received a coached facial and makeover, resulting in a glamorous evening face, suitable for the occasion of a wedding celebration. The women were thrilled.

Upon leaving the hotel, I called Susan, my sales director,

who always reveled in these spontaneous and unexpected selling opportunities. "Jane, follow up with them. Go after it! You've established a relationship with these women. You've helped them. You've touched their lives and they trust you."

"We shall see. Honestly, I think it was a one-shot deal. Just my intuition" I said.

"Now why would you say that? Jane darling, you can't think like that or you will never grow your business. Go for it!" She replied excitedly.

Truth be told, none of the three women ever became my steady customer. I followed up with them on one or two occasions, but once they returned home after the wedding, they had moved on.

Most beauty consultants do not set out to become beauty consultants. Like Susan, Barbara, an executive sales director, fell into the beauty world during a career transition. A high school English teacher from the East Coast, she took a job as a marketing manager with a company in the Midwest and found the role to be lonely. Adjusting to a different lifestyle and new office ambiance, Barbara seized on the opportunity to become a beauty consultant, not so much for the income, but to develop friendships with other women.

With her background as a teacher, Barbara became a natural in building a sales team to introduce beauty lines. When asked how beauty consultants make their money, Barbara's reply is, "Selling the product pays the bills, but teaching other women to move into leadership positions as sales directors in your unit is your future and theirs."

When further queried on her views about the state of the beauty industry, Barbara comments, "Skin wellness will never go out of style. This is your bread and butter as a beauty consultant. Glamour is the icing on the cake. There is no question that there is a lot of competition out there in the beauty and cosmetic industry. This can be very confusing and, frankly, misleading for many women. Our job is to make it all easier and affordable."

Regarding biases within the beauty industry—such as having perfectly sculpted features or being at the ideal body weight—Barbara thinks the future lies in employing models who represent all walks of life, with whom consumers can identify. This would encompass men and women of various ages and ethnic backgrounds. Before and after photos are key," she adds, saying, "they really engage people and draw them into conversations."

What did Barbara mean by *teaching other women to move into leadership positions*? A sales director such as Barbara not only sells products but manages to recruit a sales team of other beauty consultants. The recruits, in turn, set up their own individual businesses, make their own commissions, and also provide the sales director with a bonus commission from the company. This is how sales directors augment their income and create a lucrative business while moving up the company ranks.

I approached two of my customers, Keisha and Debbie. Both were stylish, progressive, and modern women for their take on the beauty industry. Keisha is a thirty-something entrepreneur and mother of three. We originally met at a vendor's event. She was promoting a line of sportswear next to my cosmetic table. By the conclusion of the event, we had become friends, and I felt comfortable enough to propose myself as Keisha's beauty consultant.

Keisha found the offer most compelling, booked an appointment, and became my loyal skin care customer. She felt that the beauty industry had been forced to become more inclusive. Nevertheless, she says, there is still room for improvement, as women need to be able to identify with the models they see gracing social media while refraining from making comparisons that lead them to fall short. Analogous to Barbara's viewpoint, Keisha felt that the beauty industry should employ models who represent a range of consumers in age, gender, and race. "We need a full gamut from all ethnic backgrounds," she observed.

Debbie is approximately my contemporary. She works for a university on a full-time basis having raised two children, now young adults. Debbie agreed with Keisha that diversity is vital within the beauty industry, but Debbie is also time conscious, opting for cosmetics that respect the consumer's schedule. Regarding product selection, Debbie felt that "the ease of use and ease of removal are vital for me in selecting a skin care regimen, as time is of the essence." Keisha and Debbie both concur that:

A beauty program should be focused on skin care rather than makeup, comprising at the very least a daily cleanser and moisturizer. The skin must feel improved as a result of following the regimen.

Beauty starts from the inside- who they are as a person defines their outward beauty. In that regard, both Keisha and Debbie espouse a holistic approach to beauty.

When asked what they look for in a beauty consultant, their responses diverge. Keisha emphasized the stylishness of the consultant, while Debbie valued the characteristics of "someone calm, understanding, and intuitive. I really don't need all that high-pressured stuff. Jane, as my beauty consultant, you exude integrity which is more important than any flashy presentation."

I circle back to my customer Keisha, who echoed Bree's earlier theme of changing lives. "If the person feels insecure about their appearance, as a beauty consultant you can help correct what is troubling them." Women are no longer washed up at fifty, sixty, or seventy years of age. Precisely when people choose to retire is in a state of flux. The term *retirement* is possibly on the verge of retirement itself as people continue to work well into their eighties and nineties, especially if they love what they do.

The beauty industry is right there in a parallel, offering the tools that extend confidence and youthfulness, and hopefully combats ageism by alleviating the feeling of being sidelined.

This leads me to comment on whether there are universal characteristics of what constitutes beauty. Frankly, it's a loaded question, and the literature is inconclusive. There are many ways a person can express their beauty, but some degree of monetary effort and maintenance will always be involved. Theorists and philosophers over time have posited that beauty is either objective, subjective, relative, or some combination thereof. Objectively beautiful persons possess the key qualities of facial symmetry, youthfulness, and a healthy glow, all quintessential attributes in the beauty equation.

Subjective beauty is the by-product of the human mind and personal taste. A rock, for example, can be beautiful to its collector and rather ordinary to the passing viewer. Likewise, newsworthy celebrities may appeal to some and be off-putting to others depending on the audience. For example, some people may have greatly admired Prince Harry and Duchess Meghan for their pluck and glamour, while others responded less enthusiastically.

Relativism, on the other hand, is culturally valued beauty. A prime example drawn from history is the ancient Chinese tradition of foot binding for women, which from a modern standpoint is horrifying. Estimated to have originated in China during the tenth century, small feet were created through a painful process of breaking the woman's existing metatarsal structure and remolding the foot into an unnatural shape. The foot's altered appearance was then a mark of delicate female beauty, and throughout the imperial age of China signified high social standing and optimal marriage eligibility.[18]

According to physician and author Dr. Dimitre Dimitrov and colleagues, "Today we live in a time when the demarcation lines and borders between cultures and traditions are melting and becoming much smaller and even disappearing. Customs that were traditional for centuries in a particular area are spreading worldwide. One may consider that global beauty is here or on its way. Additionally, new aspects of beauty, such as transgender beauty, have been discussed in the 21st century."[19]

Finally, please stop to consider that the timeless morning beauty routine is sacred, a daily opportunity to prepare for the day, to build poise, to assert an aura, akin to selecting the day's wardrobe. Yet, despite its fundamental importance, the morning routine, at least in our culture, remains private. Its end result is just the opposite: public and projected as seemingly effortless, the details of which shall never be disclosed.

CHAPTER NINE
Wrapping Things Up

You are probably curious to know how my sojourn in Connecticut ended. After two years, I was able to walk into a supermarket to meet and greet an acquaintance, my personal litmus test for feeling established in a community. I had joined a gym, and my favorite local eateries were organized in my phone under "Contacts."

The apartment was emerging into a cozy retreat, strewn with paintings, houseplants, and books. Friends, in all honesty, were mostly people I had met through beauty consulting. Customer bookings were now steady. In contrast to New Jersey, I was steps from nature in Connecticut: the Long Island Sound, beautiful lakes, rustic trails, stone walls ribboning in parallel to the leaf strewn rills, and scenic spots near the office to sit and while away your precious lunch hour. A girl could get used to this!

However, the weekly commute: weekends in New Jersey, weekdays in Connecticut, and back and forth, continued to be brutal. The only way to remain in the Connecticut practice would be to down-regulate the commuting frequency from weekly to monthly. Ideally, there would be one week per month in Connecticut completely on-site and dedicated to the care of my patients. I would cover the mandatory weekend call remotely.

One day I pitched this proposal to my practice director, whom I happened to like very much. Having emigrated to Connecticut from England, he was a brilliant clinician, and shared so many valuable insights at our weekly meetings, not only on the variety of pharmacologic approaches to the treatment of depression, but also on interviewing techniques that were intended to strengthen the doctor-patient relationship.

As anticipated, the director declined my proposal, stating that a weekly on-site presence would be a mandatory part of the work arrangement, but that he was happy to have me remain on board as a doctor in the practice. I was torn at this point and knew I would have to make a choice, a difficult commute with a steady work opportunity versus an easier commute and career uncertainty back in New Jersey.

This was, of course, prepandemic and preinsurance coverage of telepsychiatry. It would be interesting to fast forward the director's response to the current practice climate. His response might be quite different, as the pandemic has forced all of us to become more flexible in the delivery of healthcare. Who knew that as challenging as the pandemic was, the silver lining would be the convenience and capacity for reimbursable telepsychiatry, with generally happier patients and improved appointment compliance.

I carefully weighed the options and reluctantly bid farewell to that practice. One bone-chilling January morning in 2014, I packed up, closed the apartment, and moved back to New Jersey where I live and work today.

You can probably view my memoir as an unconventional journey, a mild burnout survival story, although not necessarily conceptualized as such when I started my second business. Within these pages is the suggestion to adjust to circumstances as they unfold, as we have all become more adept at managing a degree of uncertainty since the pandemic. Not knowing your next step does not imply that you are a compromised or confused individual. Quite the contrary, you can be highly functional in sorting out all of the moving parts.

There is an abundance of literature on physician burnout, but virtually little written about what constitutes milder forms of burnout. In all probability, the milder forms of burnout are likely under-reported in contrast to the more significant forms that grab public attention and potentially compromise patient care.

That said, classic burnout comprises a triad of core symptoms: emotional exhaustion, depersonalization, and a diminished sense of accomplishment. What do these terms actually mean? While fairly self-explanatory, emotional exhaustion implies the feeling of being overextended and overwhelmed by the demands of work. Depersonalization refers to a sense of indifference, perhaps a loss of compassion for the patient and tenuous connection to one's colleagues. Diminished accomplishment indicates a downplaying attitude toward one's own professional achievements, above and beyond simple modesty.[20]

While depression and burnout may overlap in symptom presentation, Dr. Lloyd Sederer, a psychiatrist and author, points out that the two are separate and "burnout should not be confused with depression. The fundamental difference," Dr. Sederer explains, "is that burnout is a reaction to ongoing and significant extrinsic stress, from conditions of work and/or the worksite." Dr. Sederer outlines work conditions in medical settings that may lead to burnout—long work hours, social isolation, exposure to death and disability, and the effects of the pandemic, noting that it is important to make the distinction because the treatment differs for each condition.[21]

Estimates of the prevalence of physician burnout were high even before the pandemic. A 2023 review of thirty cross-sectional studies yielded a burnout prevalence estimate of 6 to

99 percent. This implausibly broad range was attributed to lack of standardized definitions and assessment tools administered across a variety of settings and cultures. Interestingly, the study failed to demonstrate that the pandemic had caused an increase in the overall prevalence of burnout, except for physicians directly involved in the care of COVID-19 patients.[22]

For those medical professionals on the front end of the pandemic, there were specific stresses, adding burden to the already loaded level of burnout. These included worrying about contracting COVID, passing the virus onto others, having to work overtime, lacking adequate personal protective equipment such as gowns, gloves, face shields, and masks, and having to make morally ambiguous clinical decisions, particularly during the height of the COVID outbreaks.[23]

While awareness of professional burnout has increased since the 1970s, it was a seminal study published by the Mayo Clinic in 2014 that propelled the issue to national attention. The study found that 54 percent of physicians reported either emotional exhaustion or a sense of detachment in comparison with 45 percent during a similar study in 2011, just three years earlier. The 9 percent increase did not translate into changes in the overall increases in rates of depression and suicide among the physicians, but this served as a wakeup call to take a closer look at the medical working environment.[24]

Burnout has not only been associated with unhappy doctors but an increased risk of administrative problems, including increased medical errors, lower patient satisfaction, higher health care costs, and therefore compromised patient care.[25]

Strategies to ameliorate burnout have largely focused on improved self-care, like ensuring adequate sleep, nutrition, and exercise, limiting alcohol intake, and a healthy work-family balance, but certainly not the starting of a side business.

Dr. Thomas Zaubler, chief medical officer of the behavioral

health software company, NeuroFlow, has observed that self-care can only go so far without the systemic commitment by the institution to prevent physicians from feeling like "cogs in a wheel." Dr. Zaubler added that "health care has become highly commoditized and commercialized, sometimes with a blinding focus on a financial margin."[26]

Can anyone be a psychiatrist and a beauty consultant? Or, for that matter, can anyone be a physician and take on another role, professionally speaking? I suppose so, but not everyone is equipped to handle more than one position or professional title. Believe it or not, "by day a shrink, by night a beauty consultant" was the droll mindset I branded for myself early on, in part to humor family, friends, peers, customers, and puzzled onlookers. The phrase also became a mantra given that I hadn't completely processed how I could be operating in two such distinct worlds.

It also reinforced the need to compartmentalize the two professions, necessary for anyone handling more than one business, especially in this era of heightened regulations and media visibility. Quantifying how many doctors and other professionals have multiple careers is the subject of a future research study, especially with burnout and potential physician shortages as legitimate public health concerns.

My guess is that even with all of their unhappiness, doctors rarely step down from their medical position unless forced to by external factors beyond their control. And as previously stated, there is a need to investigate the manifestations of milder, more prevalent forms of professional fatigue and its effect on the medical landscape. Think of all the people you know, doctors or otherwise, who feel silently stuck. How do they work through their inertia in the process of considering meaningful change?

As I have inferred, the skill sets of being a doctor and beauty consultant curiously overlap. Both require compassion, self-discipline, good listening skills, flexibility, persuasiveness, quick learning, savviness and the motivation to touch other people's lives. At the end of the day, however, I believe it is the beauty consultant who must remain ever more resilient due to the enormous level of competition.

Despite periodic negative media coverage, the medical field remains highly prestigious and respected. Reflecting back on my beauty consultation with the corporate attorney, Marsha, I question whether she would have handled me differently had I been interacting with her as a doctor. That thought actually crossed my mind at the time of the consultation, and I confess that I was probably overzealous in wanting to impress her with the science of skincare.

Not that how I was treated in her office that day or how much I shared about the five strata of the epidermis really matters, but it certainly opens up the issue of how people treat each other in the broader context of our societal roles. Sometimes, interpersonal disparities can be so nuanced as to be barely perceptible.

Plus, there are market forces at play. We read about the shortages of doctors, including psychiatrists, as a heightened demand for medical services has emerged since the pandemic. According to one reputable source, burnout is in the causal pathway for physicians leaving medical practice, with a projected total shortage of 37,800 to 124,000 physicians by the year 2034.[27] In contrast, the beauty marketplace grows by leaps and bounds with an abundance of beauty brands, beauty solutions for every kind of dermatologic problem, along with beauty specialists. Competition within the beauty world, as stated, is fierce!

On some level, I have enjoyed the challenge of balancing both disciplines. Even on the toughest of days, I appreciate being a psychiatrist. It provides a feeling of fulfillment in knowing that I am helping my patients. Likewise, my hard-earned beauty business has become integrated into my lifestyle. It forces me to maintain a grounded perspective and stay connected with my customers while catching up on their lives as well as anticipating their cosmetic needs.

Table 6: Key items to contemplate for an add-on career:

- Do you have the time and motivation for a second business or career?
- How would you characterize your energy and persistence levels?
- What is your project management style? Do you work better planning things as a soloist or on a team, being spontaneous or detailed?
- Are you passionate about the second business? It must resonate with your core values.
- Do you have an adequate support team? You will only succeed if there are reliable mentors in your life helping to make you successful in your pursuit.
- Do you have adequate financial resources to launch your new venture? As the adage goes, you have to spend money to make money.
- What are your strengths? How can you use your strengths in planning and pursuing your second business?
- What are areas that you feel need improvement? Take a look within to examine possible self-doubts and stress triggers. How do you plan to manage those?
- Do not over-label yourself into a single role.
- Do not rush to relinquish your day job, at least before you allow your new venture to unfold, maybe over a span of years.

To round out the narrative, let's take time to review a few productive coping strategies, especially if you are feeling strained or burned out in your career. While this is an extremely broad topic, I would first assert that feeling restless is universal and that it can be productive, especially if the feeling leads you to think through your options. However, restlessness is not sufficient in itself to make an actual career change. That's a pretty big step and other necessary factors include motivation, stamina, a good support system, self-belief, emotional resilience, and passion for your new venture.

You can conceptually divide career modification into two components, the implicit or contemplative factor, that which lies within you—the emotions, thoughts, and values that go into setting new goals—and the explicit factors—the research, actions, and behaviors you put in the position to effect positive change. Explicit changes are naturally easier to measure, but your mindset should never be underestimated in laying down the important groundwork for change.

Virtually all of the items listed in Table 6 are contemplative and precede any definitive steps to alter your career. Your time, motivation, operative style, core values, areas of interest, support system, sense of self-identity, and strengths and weaknesses can all be seen to ostensibly lie within Prochaska and DiClemente's gold standard model of change.[28]

Cognitive barriers to change include:

- Lack of self-confidence
- Lack of belief in the new project- while your current situation isn't perfect, it is bearable and good enough
- Lack of a specific vision for what must change and how the change will unfold or be operationalized
- The need to preserve financial, vocational and role security at all costs

♡ Anticipation of negative pushback or confusion from family, friends, and colleagues pertaining to your new venture

Some of these barriers have been intermittently addressed throughout my memoir. For example, even though the patients were receiving the best care I could deliver, I nevertheless hit an impasse when I experienced a failure in popularity with some of them. At that point, my self-esteem demanded a career adjustment, the specifics of which literally plucked me out of a swimming pool one enchanted evening.

This is not the typical scenario. Many people work methodically for years to affect a career change or, for that matter, other life changes. Some of your best decisions may percolate for a long time before coming to fruition, often through thinking outside the box, through random encounters, or through being exposed to others you admire.

One or two people who come to mind have shared with me that they left their day jobs and entered training to become emergency medical technicians, after watching how first responders skillfully saved the life of an acutely ailing relative. Obviously, it took time, perseverance, and careful study to allow for the career change.

No matter how enticing the opportunity, I recommend that you keep your day job before jumping into any new venture! Also, be prepared to walk away from that venture during the negotiation phase if some aspect feels off kilter.

How many times have you walked away from a rental opportunity or apartment purchase? Maybe the property was poorly located, the walls paper thin, or you could hear the incessant barking of a neighbor's dog during the showing. Maybe the square footage was off, you did not like the kitchen layout, or you felt that the long-term investment potential was limited. Just as you trusted your real estate instincts, trust those of your career as well. Those instincts will protect and guide you.

As for self-confidence? That comes from experience and mastery. It is not innate. Nobody can ever talk you into feel self-confident. You develop confidence in those skills that you have mastered, proving to yourself that you have this.

As a private assignment, I invite you to make a column of your strengths—areas where you feel self-confident—and a column of areas where you feel self-improvement is warranted. If you are feeling particularly introspective, you can even add a third column listing stress triggers and how you plan to address those.

For example, if you happen to be unduly sensitive to feedback from others to the point where you interpret any outside remark as a possible criticism, your task would be to appraise what was actually communicated by the other party. If the comment was legitimate, take ownership of the observation and see how it may be useful. Conversely, if it was not a productive remark, let it affect you for no more than five minutes. Then drop it from your thoughts. After all, it was just one person's opinion. The more you practice this exercise, the more resilient you will become.

In the bigger picture, never second guess your well-intentioned career path. Try to avoid that downward spiral. You are on your path for your reasons and not for someone else's benefit. Look within to better understand how your choices have evolved, guide yourself accordingly with the objective to stay on track.

Turning to the second category, that of taking action, you are, of course, not obligated to take any action. If you do decide to start a new venture or pursuit, I would recommend setting manageable self-expectations, along with a realistic budget and timeline.

You can custom-design your own plan of action for career modification or, alternatively, use an existing online template.

I recently performed a casual internet search that yielded more than twenty-five action plan formats. Also termed workflow and project managers, these are more comprehensive than the standard to-do lists which typically comprise a check off column, a description of the task column, and the time deadline column. A to-do list rather than an action plan may be all that is needed to keep you on track with your goals.

An action plan has certain essential components, typically appearing as either column or row headings depending on the format design: 1) the deciding of goals, 2) a listing of actions needed to facilitate the goal(s), 3) prioritizing each action as high, medium, or low, 4) allocating tasks to others where applicable, 5) establishing a timeline for each task and 6) reviewing the status of your project or commenting about the project in a special section—expediters, obstacles and necessary modifications.

Your second assignment should you wish to move forward with a new project is to locate an action plan model that suits your style. Then, fill it in on a regular basis. After several months of documentation, compare how you are feeling now about your new project versus how you felt when it was still tucked away in your imagination. These two assignments, self-reflection and objective measurement of your accomplishments, will hopefully be productive.

Most importantly, remain curious and open to possibility. Some of your most seemingly insignificant exposures may be game changers, leading you in an entirely new direction.

One example of a random game changer for me occurred during vacation on a ranch resort in Tucson, Arizona. I was lounging at a gorgeous desert poolside when I overheard a conversation between two guests sitting near me. They were in the process of planning an upcoming community fundraiser. Their conversation was straightforward yet so harmonious.

For some reason, I began to reflect on whether to become

involved in event planning as a way of contributing to the community. Eventually, I volunteered to assemble several fundraising events with a local arts organization, the fundraising experience bolstering my organizational self-confidence, and a bonus for my later success as a beauty consultant.

Remember that you can love what you do even on the toughest of days. Reflect on how your past year or two has unfolded. Chances are that whatever setbacks you encountered were balanced by the small victories, even during the pandemic.

In conclusion, I return to being a shrink by day, and a beauty consultant by night. While that phrase is always a conversation grabber, I think we as humans are all wired to be something by day and something else by night. For a while, that mindset and my dual business arrangement were fitting, but at this juncture, postpandemic, who knows what the future may hold.

ACKNOWLEDGMENTS

I could not have accomplished writing this memoir without the invaluable assistance from the many amazing professionals on my team. There was the initial editorial guidance of Robert Schirmer who, with thoroughness and encouragement, reviewed my earliest drafts, making the changes that would point me in the right direction.

In addition, I extend my deepest gratitude to my entire publishing team including John Koehler, president and publisher of Koehler Books, and the Koehler Books editorial staff, including Danielle Koehler, Joshua Bowes, and Becky Hilliker. Thank you to Lauren Hathaway, founder of Grace Taylor PR, and Stephanie Adwar, Esq. for believing in my project, and graciously guiding me along the path to fruition. It certainly does take a village! And who knew that writing promotional blogs could be so rewarding.

I thank Mr. Brian Lowe, founder of BML Public Relations for his knowledgeable input into the effective use of publishing world publicity.

I would like to acknowledge the following colleagues who have generously lent their expertise in the field of medicine and psychiatry: Catherine Heffner, DO; Naomi Weinshenker, MD; Thomas Zaubler, MD; and Anthony Grieco, MD. I would also like to thank my colleague, Mr. Chris Calabrese, currently on track for a PhD in counseling for reviewing the available professional options in the field of behavioral health.

Within the beauty world, I would like to acknowledge Susan, as well as Barbara, both cosmetic sales directors, for each charitably sharing their perspectives on the mindful promotion of cosmetics. Susan, you forever inspire me with reminders to believe in possibility. I would like to thank fabulous Keisha and Debbie for sharing their opinions as thoughtful and discerning customers of beauty.

For support of my project during our walks and talks, I would like to thank Manita Shrestha for her perspective, and Beth Shakman Hurd whose thoughtful feedback during our walk around the Isle of Capri provided an incredibly positive boost.

Special thanks are offered to the library staffs of Morristown Medical Center as well as the Morris County Library. You are always available and reliable when I need research assistance.

To my late parents, Phyllis and Roy, your courage, honesty, and ambition made you role models beyond the imaginable. I miss you every day! To my dear brother, Bernard, your steady presence and optimism have always anchored me.

For authors Dr. Lloyd Sederer, Ann Hood, Janet Groth, and Leonard Lauder, I loved reading your memoirs! I learned so much about the technique of writing an engaging memoir. My gratitude to you.

To my peers at Bellevue Hospital, NYU psychiatry residents like me, I could not have gotten through the arduous training program without you. My salute extends to the NYU teachers and professors. During your interviewing seminars, I learned an incredible amount about building therapeutic rapport. It was a privilege to be your student.

For the magnificent cities of Boston and New York providing energy and motivation at just the right moments, thank you.

To Laurie Martin, director of Digital Content for *The*

Carlat Report, Heidi Duerr, associate editorial director, and Leah Kuntz, editor, both of *Psychiatric Times*, thank you for appreciating my writing style early on and opening up the necessary writing opportunities to broaden the craft.

To my husband Jon, my partner and best friend, thank you for always providing honest feedback and unconditional encouragement. And to my beautiful, amazing daughters, Danielle and Victoria, who keep me on track with their gentle, hybrid technique of love and generational education, thank you!

And lastly, I extend a warm appreciation to all of my colleagues and clients in my professional worlds from whom I am ever learning, along with teachers and mentors who have ever helped me with my writing projects.

If I have missed anyone, my sincere apologies!

REFERENCES

1. Groth, J, *The Receptionist*. Algonquin Books of Chapel Hill, Chapel Hill, North Carolina, 2012.
2. Harper, A. J., *Write a Must-Read*, 2022.
3. Hood, A, *Fly Girl*, W. W. Norton & Company, New York, New York, 2022.
4. Lauder, L., *The Company I Keep: My life in Beauty*, Harper Business, New York, New York 2020.
5. Sederer L., *Ink-stained For Life: Coming of Age in the 1950s, a Bronx Tale*, Austin Macauley Publishers, London, 2020.
6. Zinsser, W., *On Writing Well*, Harper Perennial, New York, New York, 1976.

ENDNOTES

1. Wikipedia, "Managed care," Accessed April 21, 2023, https://en.wikipedia.org/wiki/Main_Page; National Council on Disability, "A brief history of managed care," accessed April 21, 2023, https://ncd.gov/policy/appendix-b-brief-history-managed-care; American Medical Association, "The resource-based relative value scale, accessed April 15, 2023," https://www.ama-assn.org/about/rvs-update-committee-ruc/rbrvs-overview.

2. Verdon, D. "Physician practice owners take a 6% pay cut in 2012, other incomes relatively flat, survey says," November 25, 2013. https://www.medicaleconomics.com/view/physician-practice-owners-take-6-pay-cut-2012-other-incomes-relatively-flat-survey-says; Medical Economics

3. "Special Report," The 91st Medical Economics, 2020;97: (9): pp 12–15. (Both graphs are reproduced with permission by *The Psychiatric Times*.)

4. *Psychiatry*, "Honoring Chester Pierce with a New Human Rights Award; Your Opportunity to Participate in the Endowment Campaign," accessed April 2023, https://www.psychiatry.org/News-room/APA-Blogs/Honoring-Chester-Pierce-a-New-Human-Rights-Award; Wikipedia, "Frieda Fromm-Reichmann," accessed April 2023, https://en.wikipedia.org/wiki/Frieda_Fromm-Reichmann.

5. *Psychiatry*, "Non-Physician Scope of Practice Advocacy," accessed May 2023, https://www.psychiatry.org/psychiatrists/advocacy/state-affairs/non-physician-scope-of-practice/non-physician-scope-of-practice-advocacy.

6. Bellevue Hospital, accessed April 1, 2023, https://en.wikipedia.org/wiki/Bellevue_Hospital;

7   Allen, Woody, *Zelig*. 1983. Metro-Goldwyn-Mayer Pictures Inc.

8   Shem, S. *The House of God*. Penguin Random House, LLC, 1978

9   Wilhelm Reich (1897–1957) was an Austrian physician and psychoanalyst who emigrated to the United States in 1939 and was subsequently imprisoned in 1956 for the fraudulent claim of being able to cure cancer with his experimental Orgone box. Reich died in confinement while serving a prison sentence.

10 Wikipedia, "The Sandy Hook Elementary School Shooting," accessed May 15, 2023, https://en.wikipedia.org/wiki/Sandy_Hook_Elementary_School_shooting.

11 Matteson, J., *Eden's Outcasts: The Story of Louisa May Alcott and Her Father*, W. W. Norton & Company, 2007.

12 Dr. Otto Kernberg was an Austrian-born American psychoanalyst and clinical psychiatry professor who published in the area of personality disorders, among his books, *Borderline conditions and pathological narcissism*.

13 Romm, S. Beauty through history. Accessed May 15, 2023. Romm, S., "Beauty through history," accessed May 15, 2023, Washingpost.com/archive/lifestyle/wellness/1987/01/27; Cline Horowitz, M, ed., "Beauty and Ugliness," New dictionary of the history of ideas. 2005. Vol 1: 198–205.

14 Whitefield-Madrano, A. Face Value. The Hidden Ways Beauty Shapes Women's Lives. Simon & Schuster, 2016. pp. 1–41.

15 Cline Horowitz, M, ed., "Beauty and Ugliness," New dictionary of the history of ideas. 2005. Vol 1: 198–205; Whitefield-Madrano, A. *Face Value. The Hidden Ways Beauty Shapes Women's Lives.*

Simon & Schuster, 2016. pp. 1–41; Greene G. The Empire strikes back. The Nation, Feb 10, 1992, pp. 166–170; Cranston M. The beauty myth: how images of beauty are used against women. Book review in American Spectator. August 1991. Vol 24: 8: 36–38.

16   Hilhorst, M., "Physical beauty: only skin deep?" *Medicine, Healthcare and Philosophy*, 2002, 5:11–21.

17   *The Tennessee Tribune*, "How women's concepts of beauty are changing, Thursday, October 27–November 2, 2016; "Beauty in Ancient Times," accessed May 15, 2023, https://aetheion.com/a-brief-history-of-beauty.

18   Cline Horowitz, M, ed., "Beauty and Ugliness," New dictionary of the history of ideas. 2005. Vol 1: 198–205; Wikipedia, "Foot Binding," accessed July 3, 2023, https://en.wikipedia.org/wiki/Foot_binding.

19   Dimitrov D., Maymone M., Kroumpouzos G., "Beauty perception: a historic and contemporary review," accessed June 2023, https://doi.org10.1016/j.clindermatol.2023,02.006; Sarwer D., Grossbart T., Didie E., *Beauty and Society. Seminars in Cutaneous Medicine and Surgery*, June 2003, Vol.22:2: 79–92.

20   Alexander, L. "Burnout in physicians," New Jersey physicians & physician assistants in NetCe Continuing Education. 2017. 142:4: 1–15.

21   Sederer L., "Burnout and its remedies." *Psychiatric Times*. Sept. 23, 2022. Vol. 39:9: 1–9.

22   Alkamees A., Aljohani M., Kalani S. et al, "Physician's burnout during the COVID-19 pandemic: a systemic review and meta-analysis," 2023, Int. J. Environ. Res. Public Health. 20:4598:1–11.

23   Alkamees A., Aljohani M., Kalani S. et al, "Physician's burnout during the COVID-19 pandemic: a systemic review and meta-analysis," 2023, Int. J. Environ. Res. Public Health. 20:4598:1–11; Saatcioglu F., Cirit B., Koprucu G. The promise of well-being interventions to mitigate physician burnout during the COVID-19 pandemic and beyond. Oncology Practice. Vol 18:12: 808–815.

24   Shanafelt T., Hasan O., Dyrbye L., "Changes in burnout and satisfaction with work-life balance in physicians and the general US working populations between 2011 and 2014," December 2015, Mayo Clinic Proceedings. 90 (12):1600–6013.

25. Alexander, L. "Burnout in physicians," New Jersey physicians & physician assistants in NetCe Continuing Education. 2017. 142:4: 1–15; Seward M., Marso C., Soled D., et al, "Medicine in motion: addressing physician burnout through fitness, philanthropy, and interdisciplinary community building," American Journal of Lifestyle Medicine. Jul–Aug 2022, pp 462–468.

26. Sofair J., "Finding the beauty with a second job." Physician Leadership Journal, November/December 2017, pp. 30–33; AMA Newswire, "By sharing his burnout story, this psychiatrist sets out to help," June 15, 2023.

27. Ayre, M. "Robust claims boost practice revenues and alleviate stress," accessed August 2023, Glenwoodsystems.com.

28. https://online.yu.edu/wurzweiler/blog/prochaska-and-diclementes-stages-of-change-model-for-social-workers, accessed June 14, 2024.

www.ingramcontent.com/pod-product-compliance
Lightning Source LLC
LaVergne TN
LVHW091545070526
838199LV00002B/213